SHAPING
change

ROSS MARINO, CFP®, CeFT®
SUSAN BRADLEY, CFP®, CeFT®

SHAPING
change

how to respond
WHEN LIFE DISRUPTS
your retirement plan

Advantage

Copyright © 2021 by Ross Marino and Susan Bradley.

All rights reserved. No part of this book may be used or reproduced in any manner whatsoever without prior written consent of the author, except as provided by the United States of America copyright law.

Published by Advantage, Charleston, South Carolina.
Member of Advantage Media Group.

ADVANTAGE is a registered trademark, and the Advantage colophon is a trademark of Advantage Media Group, Inc.

Printed in the United States of America.

10 9 8 7 6 5 4 3 2 1

ISBN: 978-1-64225-208-8
LCCN: 2021901724

Cover design by Megan Elger.
Layout design by Wesley Strickland.

This publication is designed to provide accurate and authoritative information in regard to the subject matter covered. It is sold with the understanding that the publisher is not engaged in rendering legal, accounting, or other professional services. If legal advice or other expert assistance is required, the services of a competent professional person should be sought.

Advantage Media Group is proud to be a part of the Tree Neutral® program. Tree Neutral offsets the number of trees consumed in the production and printing of this book by taking proactive steps such as planting trees in direct proportion to the number of trees used to print books. To learn more about Tree Neutral, please visit **www.treeneutral.com**.

Advantage Media Group is a publisher of business, self-improvement, and professional development books and online learning. We help entrepreneurs, business leaders, and professionals share their Stories, Passion, and Knowledge to help others Learn & Grow. Do you have a manuscript or book idea that you would like us to consider for publishing? Please visit **advantagefamily.com** or call **1.866.775.1696.**

From Ross:

To all who experienced life-altering events during the pandemic.

To Jocelyne, my wife, who presses on despite countless detours.

Special thanks to my mother for continually teaching me about people and business. Your insight has shaped me more than anyone. Thank you, Mom, for always being a patient editor, irregardless of how many errors I writed.

From Susan:

I thank all the Sudden Money Institute financial planners from around the world who helped develop the body of work this book is built upon. They are changing the financial planning profession.

To Troy E. Jones, my husband and thinking partner in the adventures of life, for your support and insights and endless haikus.

This publication is designed to provide accurate and authoritative information in regard to the subject matter covered. It is sold with the understanding that the publisher is not engaged in rendering legal, accounting, or other professional services. This publication should be regarded as a complete analysis of the subjects discussed. If legal advice or other expert assistance is required, the services of a competent professional person should be sought.

This material within is intended for informational purposes only and should not be construed as investment advice, a solicitation, or a recommendation to buy or sell any security or investment product. Although we take care to ensure our data is accurate and comes from reliable sources, no guarantee is made to the completeness or accuracy of the information herein. Transitus Wealth Partners, LLC, The Sudden Money Institute®, and the Financial Transitionist Institute® do not provide legal or tax advice. Tax laws are subject to change, which can impact your financial strategy and results. Please consult with your financial, tax, or legal professional regarding your specific situation.

Investments are subject to risk, including the loss of principal. Some investments are not suitable for all investors, and there is no guarantee that any investing goal will be met. All indices are unmanaged, and investors cannot actually invest directly into an index. Unlike investments, indices do not incur management fees, charges, or expenses. Past performance is no guarantee of future results.

Please consider the investment objectives, risks, charges, and expenses carefully before investing. When considering any security for purchase, remember that the prospectus, which contains this and other information about the investment product, can be obtained from your financial professional. Be sure to read the prospectus carefully before deciding whether to invest.

CONTENTS

INTRODUCTION

Life happens. And it doesn't follow a script. Instead, it throws curveballs and forks in the road and puzzles that leave us flummoxed or altogether wrung out. A wonderful gift but far from all sunshine and roses, life conjures and places obstacles, challenges, and unexpected moments in our path that force us to make some of the most important decisions of our lives. These times of transition are tricky navigational trials, whether they be financial, family-based, or other choices.

Wouldn't it be great to always have time to sit down, reflect, and think things through clearly and strategically? Alas, that convenience rarely presents itself; instead, critical decisions often must be made at times when it's hardest to keep a level head and make the right move. Some less urgent decisions can be put off. Still, it always seems the toughest ones, the most impactful, demand an on-the-spot call, and with it comes an inevitable change of plans. Your decision ultimately impacts not only you but also everyone around you as well. Managing significant, and especially unexpected, life changes and their ancillary fallout takes its toll. Everyone experiences life-altering events, and most are the common variety, such as retirement, aging, and health decline.

Consider data like this:

- Only a third of retirees retired when they had planned to.[1]

- A 65-year-old couple retiring in 2019 can expect to spend $285,000 in healthcare and medical expenses.

- Baby boomers are receiving an unprecedented $9 trillion inheritance.

- The median 401(k) balance in the United States for ages 50–59 was $65,300.

- Sixty-eight percent of baby boomers either expect to work or are already working past age 65. Yet, the average retirement age of currently living retirees is *59.88 years old.*

- In the past 25 years, the divorce rate doubled for Americans over age 50 and tripled for those over age 65.

All of these examples and many others just like them trigger enormous, financially based life transitions. Think of it this way—everyone who is currently working will one day stop working; they will retire, develop a disability, or pass away. Whatever the scenario, we all reach a point where we are no longer working and making money. We transition from working for a paycheck to no longer working.

This transition is commonplace; very few of us work and generate income our entire adult lives. A caveat is semiretirement—today's new retirement—when we continue working as long as it remains fulfilling and we are physically able. The gist is that eventually income we are used to stops coming in, and many people are surprised at what that

---

1   "The Current State of Retirement: Pre-Retiree Expectations and Retiree Realities," Transamerica Center for Retirement Studies, accessed November 4, 2020, https://www.transamericacenter.org/docs/default-source/retirees-survey/retirees_survey_2015_report.pdf.

feels like. Preparation only goes so far, and even the most astute among us aren't entirely ready for the lifestyle change.

Preparation only goes so far, and even the most astute among us aren't entirely ready for the lifestyle change.

And so enters the tragically overlooked human side of retirement. Most people focus on the financial side, and for good reason. It's easier with a defined point of reference. Let's say you were making $5,000 a month before retirement, and once you retire, you'll receive $3,000 per month. The numbers are right there, and you can sit down and consider what that will look like. How much can you spend? Where can you cut back? Your average sixth grader can do that math.

But the human side is a mystery. You can't anticipate what retirement will be like because you've never been there before. Sure, you've dreamed about it, visualized it, and maybe even developed a plan for your new day-to-day routine. You're older and more mature and comfortable with a consistent income and budget. But that night and day change of retirement upends your usual routine and personal relationships, which can be overwhelming for many people. Indeed, retirement's human side is undefined and riddled with the unknown. The unfortunate fact is that most people don't fully prepare. After all, the freedom of retirement sounds great. It is supposed to be a relaxed, enjoyable life chapter, but there is a dark side to retirement, harboring a high percentage of depression, substance abuse, divorce, and suicide.

Why the disparity? What happens in the transition from relatively content, or at least familiar, working years to retirement? The answer lies in the financial-human dynamic.

THE FINANCIAL PLANNING CROSSROADS

Personal financial planning is, for the most part, a practice of the finite. You can approach it with objective standards, and planners can train for that accordingly. A budget shows if we're spending more than we earn, and we can quantify the financial impact of particular life events, like losing a job or death. Sounds simple enough, and as such, it's easier and certainly effective to train financial planners to help clients on the financial side.

The human element is an entirely different world, and attempting to integrate that by, say, adding another class or presentation won't cut it. CERTIFIED FINANCIAL PLANNER™ practitioners (CFP®) and their associated board have transformed the financial services industry, and we are grateful for it. They are extremely adept at examining the nuances of retirement planning, insurance, personal finance, and a host of other finance components. But the human side is much more subjective and can be very difficult to integrate, and yet it's more common today for people to want to talk about elements beyond finance. We've seen the positive effects of addressing the human side and the consequences of not doing so. Dedicated subject matter experts are doing something about it by working to train the financial community.

Through behavioral science, we know that the bulk of people's financial decision-making is influenced more by feelings than facts.

Is financial planning subjective, objective, or both? The answer, of course, is both. Through behavioral science, we know that the bulk of people's financial decision-making is influenced more by feelings than facts. A Gallup poll shows that 70 percent of decisions are emotional and 30 percent rational, but financial advisors receive little training on the emotional side. It's too "squishy," and every person is unique. The financial planning industry was built on a foundation of knowledge, with evolving processes to help people make decisions. Today we know personal financial planning is just as much personal as financial. Plenty of money to retire doesn't guarantee a fulfilling retirement. Many retirees experience depression, substance abuse, divorce, or suicide. Virtually any financial planner has clients who have struggled with a loss of identity and depression. For some, the end result was divorce. For others, suicide. The statistics are alarming but clearly reflect that the "squishy" element that drives financial decisions and related activities, questions, and behaviors is more prevalent than ever.

At this point, you may be wondering who we are. Ross Marino is a thirty-year financial industry veteran and founder of Transitus Wealth Partners based in Wilmington, NC. Susan Bradley is author of *Sudden Money: Managing a Financial Windfall* and founder of the Sudden Money Institute. The institute trains financial planners in five continents to be CeFTs (Certified Financial Transitionsists®). Our goal with this book is to shine a light on how major life events—losing a job, retirement, moving to a new home—trigger a life-altering process, which we call a transition. This process influences how you feel, how you make decisions, and ultimately your quality of life.

THE HAPPINESS PROJECT BAROMETER

In an interesting but not all that surprising twist, the project reveals that the world's highest-paid people aren't necessarily the happiest. There's plenty of data out there, and people already know that money isn't everything. But as a group, financial advisors still tend to say,

"If you have enough money, you'll be okay," and people are conditioned to believe that. To some extent money *can* buy a certain sense of satisfaction, especially for those earning more than $95,000 per year.[2] A reason.com article references Princeton University economist Angus Deaton's finding that more money can have a significant impact on our overall satisfaction with life. Indeed, it is often more challenging to feel secure and content when you struggle to pay the bills every month.

Fortunately, most of us know money is not enough; it's not what fulfills us as human beings. That's why it is critical to bring the human element of financial decisions front and center and help people with their overall well-being. Life constantly changes, but planning is indispensable to gauge your direction and make decisions that will benefit your future. It's about shaping change, the foundation of this book.

Remember that change appears in many forms throughout our lives. When your life pivots, the bigger moments often need more attention, and we want to help you lean into change and shape it rather than let change shape you. Life might disrupt your retirement plans and things might not play out the way you hoped, but you have the strength to continue growing and learning.

Life is a wonderful gift—it just won't feel like it all the time. Change is constant, and the challenge is to embrace it, lean into life events, and shape your future.

---

2   Andrew T. Jebb, et al., "Happiness, income satiation and turning points around the world," *Nature Human Behavior* vol. 2 (1), January 2018, https://pubmed.ncbi.nlm.nih.gov/30980059/.

PART 1:

A MODERN-DAY PARABLE

LIFE IN ACTION

The morning after. Still a buzz in the air from last night's party. Robert Parker turned sixty, and Marie, his bride of thirty years, outdid herself, pulling out all the stops and packing the house with family and close friends to cheer the moment.

When the crowd called for a toast, Robert raised his glass and put his arm around Marie. "You never really think you're going to be sixty, and then, wow, there you are, or, I mean, here I am. The truth is I never would have made it this far without Marie. Her understated energy and unwavering determination got me hook, line, and sinker from day one. And nothing's changed. Look at the gleam in my eyes. No, really, later on, look at the gleam in my eyes. Same as the day we met. Two college kids with a great big future ahead of them. You know what? I feel the same way right now. So here's a toast to my wife and to us all. Here comes the great big future."

True to family tradition, birthdays and other significant events are followed by reflecting on the past year and sharing thoughts on what tomorrow might look like. Marie's older sister Linda Forte has spent the night and awoken early to help clean up the mess. She joins

Marie and Robert in their newly remodeled kitchen, scrubbing dishes, putting away food, reorganizing cupboards.

"This really is a great kitchen, Rob," Linda says. "You went above and beyond."

"Thanks, Lin," Robert says. "Marie always wanted a chef's kitchen, and I could never give her one. But when I got promoted to regional sales manager and took home the bonus that went with it, I knew it was time to pull the trigger. Can't say I'm not proud of it. No kidding, that job changed my life. Or at least my kitchen."

"The keyword is bonus," Marie says. "Rob had a great year, but there's no way I would have let him tap our regular budget for something like this. It was the spark we needed. I love it. I call it our 'bonus kitchen.'"

The family is close and works well together. They have their own calendars and routines, and while life is busy, it is somewhat predictable, and they're all in tune with one another's schedules, getting together as often as possible. Everything is pretty okay with the world as the cleanup chores wind down. Timing it perfectly, Angie Forte, Linda and Marie's mother, shuffles into the room. Steeped in proud first-generation Italian lineage, she's glad to see her daughters pitch in, but she's tired and already antsy to get on with the day, specifically hitting the road to go home.

These mini family reunions are always enjoyable. When her daughters steer the conversation toward finance and other money matters, Angie wastes no time working her way into a light jacket, kissing everyone goodbye, and striding confidently out into the spring morning, straight to her car.

At eighty-three, she's still independent as ever but beginning to slow. Her family wants her to hang up the car keys for good—she sometimes forgets where she's going, and they are naturally concerned she won't find her way home. She occasionally has trouble pulling out a word she should know, which makes her anxious. It happened just the other day. Angie's mother taught her to sew at a very young age, and she can still almost do it with her eyes closed, but a few days ago (or was it yesterday?), she told Marie her machine was broken. Marie asked what machine, but Angie couldn't remember a name she has seen and worked with most of her life.

Despite a slow decline, however, she makes it home, and Robert rejoins Marie and Linda in their customary chat. Like most people, they all hope for comfortable, worry-free, financially secure futures, and today is kind of a wake-up call.

"So Rob is sixty," Linda says, "and the next thing you know, we'll all be retired, and what are you two thinking about that? Are you ready?"

"Kind of. We don't have a grand financial plan in place, but we're not doing nothing," Marie says.

"Save more, spend less, don't do anything stupid," Rob says.

Basic financial planning, and they've been doing it all along—Robert is locked into a solid career making good money. He isn't all that worried about tomorrow, thanks in large part to Marie's sharp saving and investing mind.

"There's more to it than that," Linda says. "Will you have enough to live the way you want or the way you've been living? And even if you do, what will it be like—I mean, really be like—when Rob retires. Will you want to be around him twenty-four hours a day?"

Marie is the CEO of the house and their finances, but Robert's string of job changes early in his career caused a streak of nagging concern. She's great about squirreling away money, but Linda has hit a nerve. Marie always worries "what if?"

"You ready for twice the husband and half the income?" Linda says.

Everybody laughs, but Marie knows that Linda, older than her by three years, has done amazingly well saving for retirement. And the more she thinks about it, Marie realizes she and Robert don't have what her sister has. Marie is the deep thinker in her relationship with Robert and knows well that money is only part of the retirement equation. A very human element also exists that carries as much, if not more, importance. She is dogged by legitimate and not uncommon unease: Robert retires and loses work and his identity, she loses the freedom of choosing her personal time activities, and their financial abilities drastically change.

"The truth is, I'm happy," Rob says. "I'm working hard and not all that excited about retiring. I love my job, where my career is at. I'm vital to the company; I like the work and the challenges. I like my colleagues. I'm doing work that matters, and I feel like I'm where I should be at this point in my life. And I don't feel any older, even though I'm sixty. Why should I retire or even think about it? I'm in a good groove, and I plan to keep on going."

He does have a five-year timeline in his head but hasn't shared it with Marie. They've talked about retiring in five years, but he doesn't want to discuss it; he's making great money and enjoys being successful, especially after so many early career struggles. He's crushing it at work, and it feels great; in fact, he abhors the idea of a retirement countdown in spite of everyone around him thinking otherwise.

Robert's five-year countdown coincides with Medicare eligibility, but he would be subject to a reduced Social Security benefit. Many people feel the "right time to retire" is when they qualify for both programs. However, Medicare eligibility begins at age sixty-five for Robert. But taking Social Security at age sixty-five instead of sixty-seven would reduce Robert's monthly benefit by more than 13 percent.[3]

Many people can't wait to say goodbye to work, but Robert is comfy where he is. Why, then, isn't he sharing his thoughts with his wife? Is he worried about losing his happiness? Will it add to Marie's worry?

THE FINANCIAL PLANNING LIGHT BULB

Right about the time Marie's financial worries are redlining, Linda comes to the rescue, or at least sheds light on a new idea.

"Marie, listen, this is the perfect time to meet with a financial planner to make sure everything you're doing is on track and you don't have any regrets down the road," Linda says. "I know you, and I know Rob. You don't feel secure about this next part of your lives. Rob's like, 'Hey, no worries, everything's going to be okay.' But that's not you. So talk to a planner. I know an excellent CFP. Jennifer Rose. Aren't you curious about how she could help you?"

Marie is curious. She's tuned into the money ingredient and its role in life's complex recipe. She reads investment books for fun and is hooked on robo-advisor websites. She gets a kick out of plugging numbers into virtual finance portals to see what comes out; some recommendations aren't consistent and much is confusing, but she knows what they have to work with, and her keen budget sense is keeping the household ticking along.

It's true that Robert has a general "it'll all work out" view of the whole thing (Marie admits she envies that sometimes) and that he's only focused on his job, not how much money they'll have when he

---

3   "Benefit Reduction for Early Retirement," Social Security Administration, accessed
     November 4, 2020, https://www.ssa.gov/OACT/quickcalc/earlyretire.html.

retires. But Marie weathered their income roller coaster for years. Her instinct says to build up enough funds to cement a safe future where they can pay the bills and have a little left over.

But what is "enough money"? Every website seems to spew out a different number—one website says you should have enough cash in savings to cover three to six months of expenses; the book she's reading says one to two years. That's a huge difference! She's confused, but she's relatively-almost-just-about confident they don't have enough right now. Another five years of "saving like I always have" and they should be in good shape. Or will they?

Retirement can throw a wrench into the works; changes in routine and relationships have a tremendous effect on the current state of things, as well as how tomorrow unfolds.

Marie doesn't bother to ask Robert what he thinks. She probably should, but he trusts her, and that dynamic has driven their relationship for years. He jokes that when it comes to money, he makes it and she takes it. She says if she didn't take it, he'd spend it. However, retirement can throw a wrench into the works; changes in routine and relationships have a tremendous effect on the current state of things, as well as how tomorrow unfolds.

Just ask Linda. She's sixty-two and still hard at work as an HR manager. Married with children at one time, her ex plunged into a midlife crisis in his early forties, they soon divorced, and she raised their children as a single parent. She went back to her maiden name as soon as her divorce was final because she had a sense of what was to come: her ex would rarely see the kids and would miss plenty of child support payments, leaving Linda to shoulder the burden. And that's exactly what happened. But she sacrificed here and worked harder there and held it all together. Sometimes paycheck to paycheck, other times day by day, but she made it and did a great job raising her kids, two boys, who are now young adults living full lives and living them well.

However, one snag in the works is she had no substantial retirement savings before her husband left so there was a lot of catching up. The silver lining is life taught her how to prioritize and be very frugal and it's all paying off—she makes good money and saves aggressively, which has inspired thoughts of retiring. She spends more time with friends playing pickleball, cycling, or taking weekend trips and thoughts simmer in her head about what retirement life could look like. Like her sister, Linda is in the midst of a major life transition.

THE FOUR STAGES OF TRANSITION

Simply defined, transition is movement from what was to what is and looking forward to what will be. You can't change what was and must accept what is, but what will be is yet untold. That is your opportunity to shape change. We all go through many periods of transition throughout life; some might be like Linda's drastic change to being a single parent, while others might be as simple as opening your first checking account as a teenager. Whatever the scenario, transition happens in four stages:

1. Anticipation
2. Ending
3. Passage
4. New normal

Marie and Linda are both in the first stage, anticipating something that hasn't happened with a timeline and scenario yet unknown. This heavily influences their everyday thinking and decisions. It is a tricky place to navigate, as there can be simultaneous feelings of invincibility and hopelessness. The promise of a financial windfall, for example, can be exciting and inspire feelings of invincibility. A loss, however—divorce or death of a loved one—can be devastating and lead to hopelessness. Fortunately, you can steer toward calmer waters by taking a deep breath, slowing down, and not rushing into any big decisions.

Marie finds herself looking at numbers all the time, and she's worried; it won't work if Robert can't earn (and they can't save) at their current rate for another five years. Maybe she should have worked part-time somewhere to learn new skills and establish a network.

Linda is in a better place financially, but she's staying smart and watching for attractive retirement packages at work. She regularly talks with a financial planner to keep a tangible plan in place. She doesn't want to make any sudden moves, but there are so many questions. What if I retire in five years? Earlier? Is that realistic or borderline reckless? What penalties are incurred for accessing funds? How does it impact Social Security?

Linda needs to know what she can afford before spending too much time dreaming about life on a retirement beach somewhere. She dives headlong with her planner into the numbers deep end. She's still in her peak earning years, so retiring early not only eliminates earning potential, but it also reduces Social Security benefits, while working another five boosts her primary insurance amount (PIA). She also won't be eligible for Medicare for three more years. Private medical insurance is expensive, but as is the case with most people in the modern workforce, her employer subsidizes the cost and she has no real grasp of what out-of-pocket expense looks like.

NOW, SOON, LATER

Jennifer Rose, Linda's financial planner—along with many in the same role—recommend a now, soon, later strategy. Prioritizing is one of the primary advantages of partnering with a planner. Linda's immediate focus is the "now"—she should request medical insurance options and Social Security estimates and gather all of her financial information to create a current budget.

Looking ahead, the soon stage includes picturing what retirement could look like from a personal, not financial, perspective. What do you want to do, with whom, where, and why? Focusing on the why is critical to discovering what matters most to you. Many people still work even though they don't need the money. Just because someone could afford to retire doesn't mean they should. Each person needs to consider both sides of retirement, human and financial.

Even further ahead, Linda will enter the later stage, where she meets and discusses early retirement scenarios with her planner. With plenty of time to think things through and current data at hand, they can look closely at numbers. Retirement initially sounded risky when reviewing Social Security and medical insurance data, and she only thought about what she was retiring *from* (work), not what she was retiring *to* (freedom).

One element in her favor is her company has hinted a new round of retirement packages may be coming soon, and this fuels her anticipation stage. Close association with the CEO and other upper management gives her access to inside goings-on and fuels a time of self-selection, making professional and sound decisions based on personal circumstances.

In the past Linda felt trapped by self-selection as a mother, corporate worker, and wife, but she doesn't regret her decisions; she'd make the same ones again. Her priorities were raising her children and working hard, and she did these things. Now she is in a stage of palpable anticipation, imagining the retired life, getting more excited every day. As she moves through the anticipation stage, preparation becomes more strategic, and she sees the balance of possibilities shift from frightening to enticing. She's not a victim of circumstance anymore; she can make decisions when they fit best and make the most sense, leveraging her habit of trending toward the proactive. Interestingly, her sister and Robert are the opposite, living more reactive lives and then scrambling to keep up and manage change.

Angie, on the other hand, doesn't talk much about money at all. Her husband didn't either, nor did their generation as a whole. They both grew up on the heels of the Great Depression, and that shaped their views on money: be frugal and don't borrow. Her husband made it through high school (barely) but didn't go to college; he spent most of his working life as a factory union hand and retired with a decent pension that helped send their kids to university studies. When he died, Angie found herself alone and struggling at first, but an inheritance on her parents' passing was plenty to pay off her mortgage and infuse retirement funds.

She doesn't think much about money these days; the time is fast approaching when she won't be able to live on her own, and with that comes almost daily thoughts of aging's insatiable grip. She's lonely, widowed five years, and her circle of friends continues to evaporate— they either move away or pass away, and Angie feels more isolated by the day. Maybe she'll move in with Linda (who doesn't know her mother is considering this yet) and spend more time with her daughters. It could be like old times, when the whole family piled in the car to go somewhere, everywhere, rolled down the windows and sang old Italian songs. Could it be like this again?

Marie and Linda remember well those heady days of youth and pass away another hour or so of post-birthday decompression as Robert stealthily departs to tinker in the garage. There's still a flow to things but perhaps tinged with an air of trepidation. The unknown has a way of sneaking into your mindset and upsetting life's apple cart. This family's status quo might be ripe for change; how they prepare and adapt will shape the outcome.

SCENE 2:

UPHEAVAL

Time passes, life percolates, and all is well. And then, at age sixty-one, the ground shakes without warning.

"Hi, Jim."

"Morning, Rob. Come on in; take a seat."

It's Robert's usual Friday morning meeting in the conference room with Jim Andrews, his division vice president. No big deal. Small talk. Sales numbers. Goals to meet. Back to work.

"I'm going to get right to it," Jim says. "We've been surveying our departments and have decided a reduction in force is necessary to continue profitable operations. A number of positions have become redundant, and yours is one of them. I'm sorry, Rob. We're eliminating your position."

Robert feels like he's been hit by a train and sits there in absolute shock, beside conference room windows overlooking the town park, where families and young couples and boisterous children frolic in the sunshine, apparently without a care in the world. Robert suddenly feels a swell of longing to be down there with them, barefoot in the grass and far away from what has just happened.

He thought he was rocking it at work, and his sales numbers told the tale. He's a smart guy and saw changes in his industry, but they seemed a distant concern, nothing that would affect his department. In fact, he recently read a company article about their Australian division's adoption of new technologies that made many positions expendable, redundant. He's been in the business world long enough to understand most employees have little visibility beyond their own departments, but he is well aware of new technologies and trends that can eliminate jobs, divisions, even entire companies overnight.

He also knows the company CEO and fellow executives have a different perspective and focus on business operations and understood what was happening in Australia, but he never expected it to happen in his division. He was wrong.

Robert has been thrust into the ending stage of transitions. Like most people in his position, he never thought something like this would happen to him. He was sensible enough to know it *could* happen, of course, but it's still a shock. One day he was at the top of his game and an important cog in his company; the next day, he's essentially a wrench in the works and booted.

What will he tell Marie? His mind spins like a whirlpool at sea; he's nauseous and struggling to process what he has just heard. *I can't believe it. How can they eliminate my position? I'm in the middle of a project. I have important meetings next week and months of work waiting on big decisions. People count on me; I can't just walk away. Don't the managers realize what I contribute to the company?*

It's the punch you don't see coming, the shock of what you don't expect, that hurts the worst. It feels "sudden" when a parent or relative passes away, even if they're pushing ninety-seven and in hospice care. But you still don't expect it, just like you don't expect your job to end tomorrow, a spouse to die, a divorce—ending without anticipation. In

Robert's scenario, job terminations are a reality of business and happen all the time, but he didn't spend the days thinking his world might end tomorrow. That's not the way to be successful as an employee, parent, child in everyday life.

But his financial world in its current iteration *did* end, and he knows how important his income was to his identity, Marie, and their future together. After graduating from college, he had nine different jobs, many at smaller companies with few benefits, before finally landing at a company with a 401(k) option at age thirty-one. Was it too late to start saving? Job-hopping, having children, and paying for their college put a hit on retirement savings, and his inner dialogue is on constant rewind: *Did I do the right thing? Did we save enough? What is enough, anyway? Should we have tapped into retirement savings to pay for college? How will I replace my income?*

He has managed to accumulate modest savings but not enough for a comfortable retirement. He's devastated and feels like a failure and doesn't want to tell Marie. They were preparing for something else; will they manage to adapt?

GUT PUNCHES AND REALITY CHECKS

Robert's HR personnel come into the conference room and go through the motions of trying to help, walking through job separation steps and outlining options for continuing a semblance of employee benefits, job placement assistance, or help updating his resume.

Updating my resume? Job placement support? Robert feels like he's hearing another language and is filled with fear, anxiety, and a sense of doom. One minute he's confident he'll find another job, and the next he pictures the unemployment line—a flurry of gut punches pummels optimism. HR reps are talking, but he doesn't really hear them and can't process their words. They have everything in writing and hand him a packet of information that looks like "goodbye" sealed in a tidy little envelope. He is no longer part of this company.

They ask if he has any questions, but he's not interested in talking to anyone right now. There is only fear and uncertainty. *What will I do now? How can I replace my income at this age? What if my severance runs out before I find a new job? I'm up against technology and people twenty years younger who will work for half the pay. I should have known this could have happened and prepared, maybe saved more or worked toward another promotion.*

Robert packs a few things in a box and walks out the door of his office for the last time. Shoulders sagging and head low, he sinks in behind the wheel of his luxury SUV. *How am I going to afford this car?* He stares out the window for several excruciating minutes and then takes the long way home.

The moment he walks in the door, Marie knows something is wrong. Robert's face is devoid of emotion, and he is concerningly quiet. She gives him a minute to "come to life," but he doesn't.

"What's going on?" she says.

He avoids eye contact. "Apparently, I'm redundant." He looks out the back window with a thousand-yard stare. He can barely hold it together. "I got fired today."

Marie freezes. Can't believe what she just heard. "What? Fired? They fired you? I don't understand. What happened, Rob? Tell me what happened."

He shakes his head and trembles a bit but can only manage, "I'm sorry."

Marie has so many questions but keeps them to herself for now. Her mind races in time with her husband's—she remembers well their early years of marriage, when Robert had a new career every few years.

Despite lighter episodes of worrying now, she thought their roller-coaster financial days were over. The evening drags on with a pall, and she can't help but think back to 2007 to 2009, the scariest chapter in their marriage, when markets crashed and people everywhere lost their jobs. Robert was one of them, and with little saved at the time for retirement, she moved some of their investments to cash. They couldn't afford to lose what they had; his 401(k) made up the bulk of their savings, and if he didn't find another job quickly, they could lose their house.

She checked account balances daily (or more often) and saw years of savings wiped out in a few months. She planned to wait until things settled down before reinvesting, but of course once everything else settled down, the markets were higher and they ended up with less of a financial cushion than they would have had she left things alone. The professionals always say don't panic, but that's exactly what she did. The silver lining, however, is Marie committed fully to learning about sensible financial planning.

We can't afford mistakes like that, she told herself. *I need to be better prepared next time the world turns upside down.*

With a Friday evening routine clouded by dark moods and a train wreck workday, Robert and Marie wander about the house without speaking much, take a walk, and eventually just turn the lights off on the day. Sleep will be fleeting—their entire lives as they knew them having abruptly ended.

INTROSPECTION

Saturday morning, a haze of confusion. Robert wakes and for a couple of fleeting seconds believes everything is still even keel. Then it hits him that the life he knew and loved—his job, office, coworkers, lifestyle—

ended yesterday. There's no going back. His world of demanding schedules and intense activity has screeched to a dead stop with no warning and no direction. He has gone from employed to unemployed, valuable to redundant. His very foundation has crumbled.

With major life events like this, everything you believed in, what you built upon, your security—it all feels shattered. You've been motoring along with a mindset that your most valuable asset is the ability to generate income, and the general outlook among successful people is "With a marketable skill set and my health, I can recover from a setback, and it'll all work out." But Robert has a proven and highly marketable skill set and good health but no job. Being suddenly laid off is a moment that shakes your faith to the core—the foundation you've believed in for years has just gotten ripped out from under you. Keep working, build your skills, apply them, take care of yourself—it's been your entire world every day for a decade, two decades, or three. You always did what you thought were all the right things. Now what?

Robert and Marie's "now" becomes a crisis in confidence. We all go through it, and usually with it comes a spiral into "what if." What if I can't get another job or one that pays what I made before? Robert doesn't know it, but this mental crisis plagues Marie all weekend as well. She tries to put on a brave face but can't keep it there. Her mind reels. *Robert might not know the numbers, but I do, and this is not good. Let's just get through the weekend. There's nothing we can do right now. I don't need to panic.*

The self-talk doesn't help. She can't help but worry about what will happen if Robert can't replace his income or even part of it. Yes, he has experience and industry relationships and he's reasonably healthy, but none of that seems to matter today because he got fired. She doesn't feel like doing anything all weekend and even avoids answering the phone. She has always been Robert's financial orchestra leader but feels deflated now, with no band to lead and stranded at a crossroads without signs.

BLUE MONDAY

Robert and Marie both felt paralyzed over the weekend, walking in circles, not talking or sleeping much. In fits and starts, Robert thought he'd be ready to move forward when the week started, but it hasn't worked out that way. For the better part of twenty-five years, Robert had a Monday morning routine. Now he has no idea what to do. He doesn't remember ever feeling this confused and lost. He's not depressed, at least not yet; it's more like a full-body numbness. He lies in bed for a few minutes, his mind pawing away cobwebs, and then it hits him: *I need to figure this out, get my butt moving and get a job.*

He knows Marie is worried sick, so he dons his game face and says he already has ideas for meetings and calls, but the truth is he doesn't really know where to go, whom to call, or what to do. Can't just sit at home, though, so Robert kisses his wife goodbye, grabs his iPad, and heads out to a coffee shop across town. His first call is to the HR department at his now former employer. The company has a traditional procedure with terminated employees, but he didn't fully process everything the HR rep shared with him on Friday; he needs to go through it again and listen closely.

His mind hangs in there for a minute or two before drifting well off track. *It's Monday, and I'm supposed to be at my desk attacking the week. Now I'm listening to someone from HR who still has a job—apparently they aren't redundant. I need to focus on what they're saying.*

The call is informative but far from encouraging, and Robert struggles to maintain composure and energy to navigate when he doesn't even know which way to go. He starts by calling friends and colleagues, and while they are sympathetic and shocked, they're busy at work and short on time.

Good luck, Robert; we wish you the best.

Early afternoon. He's still in a haze but knows he has to keep moving. He remembers reading somewhere about the fight, flight, or freeze responses to challenging events, and for him the choice is simple: fight, press forward, work hard, and *everything will be fine.*

He plunges into online searches for headhunters and thinks back to colleagues who lost their jobs a few years ago. Some never managed to replace their income, while others retired early but weren't happy. Maybe they missed working, the timing wasn't right to retire, or they didn't have "enough" money.

Robert is in an entirely different and altogether uncomfortable place. He plods through job posting sites and suddenly realizes his resume is expired like a loaf of moldy bread. *Why didn't I do that over the weekend? HR said they could help with it. I should've taken advantage of that. Get your head in the game, Rob!*

He realizes he's not his usual self, and that only fuels already rampant fear and anxiety. Sure, he has interviewed for jobs before, but he's older now and the job market is much more competitive, rife with the threat from a stable of younger talent.

For thirty days this routine replays with no sign of change. Robert can't find a single attractive option locally. Will he have to look for something out of town and commute a long distance? He's okay with being away Monday to Thursday if necessary, but he needs to be home for weekends. Is this even possible? He has executive friends in this scenario, and they seem to be content, happy, making adequate money and maintaining solid family relationships. But Robert feels like he's on a treadmill with no off switch. He wants to believe things will work out, that he and Marie will be just fine, but how?

ADJUSTING TO NEW SURROUNDINGS

It's time to readjust. Headhunters suggest lowering his bar and not expecting so much; replacing his previous income isn't easy, is difficult to achieve, and might never happen. His attitude has to change as well. He needs an energy boost, a reason to want "lesser" jobs with perhaps lower pay. Switching gears to look for local opportunities quickly reveals he is overqualified, and he's unsure any companies will hire someone his age.

Robert's severance package will keep them going for a while, so they're not desperate yet, but he's clinging to the edge, floundering under a cloud of unknowns. Natural human instinct drives his desire to protect what he and Marie had in place and their plan for the future. *What I thought was no longer is, and I have no idea what "it" is will look like. But I have to do whatever I can to get us back on track.*

He's not handling it well, and as the list of potential jobs shrinks, so does his confidence. He is more anxious, less active, and gains weight. He moved around a lot as a sales manager, regularly notching ten thousand steps a day. Now he's lucky to see three thousand. The occasional beer at dinner becomes two, and a restless night's sleep is the norm.

He simply doesn't understand his new surroundings. Losing a job at age forty-two is entirely different than losing a job when you're sixty-one. As is the case with most major life transitions, you have no idea what it will be like until you're in the middle of it, "walking a day in their shoes." People can offer advice and cheerleading all day long, but a lack of direction and understanding only muddies already murky waters. Robert can't even grasp a headhunter's recommendation to lower his sights. A month ago, he was looking toward a bright future; today he's trying to recreate the past and replace his income, and he can't even conjure a vision of what his next job might be. It's only fear, shock, and loss.

Robert and Marie receive plenty of well-intentioned but often contradictory "advice" from friends. One day it's "Take the time to reflect and think about your future and what's best for you," and the next it's "You're not getting any younger; find a job now. Forget about optimal, and think about acceptable."

Robert soon understands they will need to accept that life won't be what they thought it would. They have to protect what they have as much as possible, including future income. He gains a glimmer of focus and realizes his timeframe (for what?) is three to five years and that many companies are not interested in hiring someone with a shorter time horizon. Robert has been in business long enough to understand age bias in hiring, even though age discrimination is illegal.[4]

Some employers believe younger employees cost less and will potentially stay longer. Even if a starting salary is fixed, regardless of age, benefits have variable costs. If the employer pays for all or part of either medical or life insurance, the cost for a sixty-year-old may be substantially higher than for a forty-year-old. Length of employment is potentially longer for a forty-year-old than for a sixty-year-old.

Part of Robert's big picture is he has to stop thinking about what he could lose. Losing a job with above-average income and lots of friends at work was already a blow. It's tough to imagine letting anything else go, but after a few months, he realizes there's no chance for a lateral move in his industry or a similar one. He can't replace what he had, and his income will be considerably less going forward; that's all there is to it. He needs to let go of his "ideal job" and stay open to other, more realistic possibilities. The next job might require

---

4   Kenneth Terrell, "Face-to-Face Job Interviews Can Trigger Age Bias," AARP, January 13, 2020, https://www.aarp.org/work/working-at-50-plus/info-2020/job-interviews-age-discrimination.html.

travel or be in a completely different industry, or he might return to sales in a lower-rung capacity.

Robert is in a place of self-discovery, and answers to his questions and concerns are continually evolving. What he sees as critical to protecting today might be entirely different in six months. For example, income seems most important right now, but through self-discovery, he could learn something else holds more value.

In the meantime his routines and relationships have changed dramatically, and this is often the most challenging part of any life transition. Robert's days are now filled to the brim with job-searching, networking, and regular exercise. He stays in touch with a few of his former coworkers but misses the social interaction. The significance and satisfaction of seeing everyone at the office played a more significant part in his life than he realized, and he wants to find ways to stay connected with more friends and, of course, have quality time with his wife.

He always expected they would have plenty of time together when he retired, and if a new job requires travel, that means less "we" time. He is emerging from the cocoon of shock and fear, and now that he has clearer vision, it's the ideal time to leverage this (hopefully) short life chapter without a full-time job commitment.

TRANSITION FATIGUE

Transitions take time and energy. It's easy to feel over-whelmed and exhausted. There are at least six areas of life affected by prolonged transitions.

1. **Cognitive:** Decreased concentration and organiza-tion and the inability to complete tasks. People often feel their thoughts are "all over the map." The odds of making rational decisions are slim because their ability to calmly contemplate the full range of options has suffered.

2. **Emotions:** A sense of powerlessness and helpless-ness is a clear indication someone is overwhelmed and cannot envision a positive way to handle their situation. Other emotional changes include heightened irritabil-ity, decreased self-confidence, and loss of interest in usual activities.

3. **Behavior:** Classic signs of transition fatigue include self-medicating (alcohol, drugs, food, etc.), procrasti-nation, and neglect of household tasks and paperwork. People often report that they are spending more time engaging in mindless diversions such as television, computer games, or even gambling.

4. **Physical:** Be aware of changes in sleep pattern, exhaustion, and loss of appetite or weight gain. Be conscious of an increase in minor aches and pains. These problems can be exacerbated by accompany-ing behavioral changes, including poor diet and a lack of sleep.

5. **Work:** Fatigue is fairly obvious at work. Watch for decreased productivity, lack of follow-through, avoiding or limiting communication, and increased anxiety about the future.

6. **Relationships:** Signs may include social isolation, increased irritability, or uncharacteristic clinginess. Because of overwhelming evidence that social support is crucial for successfully getting through stressful times, people must resist the temptation to isolate themselves for extended periods of time.

A STEP FORWARD

Robert intentionally connects with other guys in town and volunteers for a few events at his church. Those events lead to others like them. Soon he is a regular volunteer at local charities, which is a great networking boost, as larger employers are often active in area nonprofits. Hopefully, he can find opportunities to rub shoulders with a key contact at one of the companies on his wish list. Through the volunteering process, he learns he really enjoys helping out. People appreciate his efficiency and dedication to a task. He's still without a job and continues to search, but at least now he has a purpose, and it feels good—a tremendous step toward a future with substance. Robert is intuitively replacing the components of work by creating a new version of routine, social interaction, challenging activities, and measuring progress, even though it's different every day.

While rays of positive moments are nice to see, it's challenging staying busy when you're used to working north of fifty hours a week.

Robert fills gaps in this new iteration of a schedule the best he can, and instead of zoning out in front of the television, he soon finds himself binge-listening to podcasts on various subjects. He is captivated by the digital drama and unexpected storylines and learns something new with every episode.

Best of all, in a palpable moment of clarity, Robert understands the importance of rhythm in his life and how it connects to and is influenced by changes. His rhythm was significantly disrupted when he lost his job, starting with his *routine*. He spent twenty-five years getting up early, driving to work, logging ten-plus hours, evenings at home with Marie, and recharging on weekends. The *social* component comprises loss (missing his friends at work) and gain (more time with Marie). The *challenging* element is Robert loved problem-solving, making critical decisions, and managing a team at work, and he doesn't have that now. He has also lost *measurable* benchmarks of hitting sales goals at work and helping people around him and the company succeed. While intense and stressful at times, these activities and everyday practices energized him and made him feel alive. Having a purpose, feeling productive, and achieving something are fulfilling.

> *People in rhythm attempt to respond thoughtfully to disruptions in life. But people who are struggling often react emotionally.*

THE INNER WORKINGS OF RHYTHM AND STRUGGLE

When life changes, people are thrown out of their rhythm, and tend to struggle. People in rhythm tend to have clarity, are resilient and energized. But people who are struggling can feel confused, hopeless, and fatigued.

When applied to decision-making, psychologists (and others) discuss it in terms of responsive versus reactive modes. People in rhythm attempt to respond thoughtfully to disruptions in life. But people who are struggling often react emotionally.

As psychologist Rick Hanson writes in *Hardwiring Happiness*, responsive mode is "your natural resting state ... the foundation of psychological healing, everyday well-being and effectiveness, long-term health, fulfilling relationships, and the highest reaches of human potential." In responsive mode, you can pause in a moment of stress and then carefully consider your next move.

This is the moment of choice where you have agency of, or some level of control over, your behavior and even your stress response. Your prefrontal cortex remains online and can make decisions that serve you. Reactive mode, roughly speaking, is when you allow your amygdala to dictate what happens. Once the amygdala is in the driver's seat, fear-based decisions and other versions of survival-based decisions are the most likely outcome.

> Being responsive takes time as you contemplate what has occurred. Reacting happens in an instant. A person in reactive mode doesn't consciously choose how they react; they just react.

Change often means loss, and since people naturally focus on what matters most (what they don't want to lose), it's only natural that the act of protecting is such a critical life component.

This was Marie's mindset when she met with Jennifer Rose, the financial planner Linda had recommended when Rob turned sixty. It was a casual meetup in a coffee shop—as opposed to an official family financial conference in Jennifer's office that both Robert and Marie would attend. For Marie, it was a chance to gather information—and blow off steam.

"We needed five more years of working and saving, and we didn't get it," Marie says.

Jennifer has handled this issue with clients before. She understands that the human and financial aspects of retirement planning are equally important. "I see how that might cause some anxiety."

"My anxiety has turned to fear. I want to protect my home, my family, our future. I know people the same age as me and Rob who lost their jobs, and they had to downsize or move to another town. It turned their lives upside down and put a lot of stress on their marriages. I don't want that to happen to us. That's the fear part."

"I understand. That's a real fear you're feeling, no doubt. So let me frame it a different way. Would you give up your house for a few years if it meant protecting your marriage?"

Marie's answer is instant, instinctive. "Of course I would."

"You just moved from protecting to letting go. And that's part of managing these life transitions. You figure it out and adapt. Those kinds of major decisions may or may not be part of your future. That's something we can figure out together when and if the time comes."

"What about my kids? We have twin boys, twenty-seven, and a twenty-five-year-old daughter. They all have independent lives, so they're okay. But I want them to know we'll be okay too. Except I don't really believe it myself yet."

"Why is that?"

"I'm attached to the life I had, to the routine. It's a big change having Rob around the house. I'm wondering what he's thinking, what he's feeling, if he's okay. Does he want to tag along with me all day? Does he expect me to stop doing what I've been doing all these years and spend time with him?"

"What do you think about asking him?"

"I don't know. I guess I'm confused. I've been the CEO of the house for years, and now I'm not. I mean, I'm not the only adult who's home all day. I don't feel like I can make all the decisions about meals and chores and projects by myself. It has to be a team effort from now on. That means I have to let go of some of my freedom, and I don't like the idea of that. The normal daily schedule won't revolve solely around my priorities anymore."

"Your 'me' time has turned into 'we' time—not the retirement you'd planned on."

"Exactly. Plus, I'm the money manager, and some unnecessary expenses have to go or I can't make ends meet. When Rob's nine-month severance runs out, the budget just won't work. It's just a matter of time before we're dipping into savings to cover our bills."

Marie doesn't want to look at financial websites anymore; with Robert's income and their 401(k) strategy, the numbers just don't work. Robert can't retire yet and needs a job, but if he gets one that doesn't allow them to save, the situation won't be much better. Marie feels overwhelmed. She's always been frugal, but how can she create a viable budget without enough income? She worries about birthday and Christmas presents for the kids, unexpected home repairs, even going out to eat. She was always the financial rock, figuring things out, but now faces an identity crisis; she doesn't know what she has to work with and begins to lose confidence. She relied on Robert to make money, and he relied on her to make the money work. Now everything they knew has been derailed. He's not making money, and she doesn't know how that can work.

Uncertainty can be challenging to overcome. You feel smart and confident when everything is going fine. That's normal. But when you realize you have no idea what to do next or how to figure things out (lack of competence), confidence plummets.

FAMILY MATTERS

While Marie comes to grips with forming new routines and relationships, her sister offers much-needed support. Linda knows what's going on and is worried. She sees it all the time—reduction in force (RIF), which is normal in the business world but a life-altering blow to workers. Companies restructure, merge, sell off divisions, and even close. Linda digs into her network on Robert's behalf but to no avail for now. She continues encouragement, but his ego and confidence are suffering; it's time to sit down and explain what she knows.

A Saturday morning with coffee in Robert and Marie's "bonus" kitchen is the ideal setting for the family conversation Linda knows it's time to have.

Angie has spent a few days there as well, helping Marie and lending support in her own way. She isn't sure about Robert's bandwidth to adjust to being at home so much; he's built for work, always has been, and she notices Marie keeps saying they'll "figure it out." But Angie can tell Robert doesn't feel the same and sees he is struggling despite

Change impacts people beyond the person experiencing the change, and the closer you are to that person, the stronger the ripple effect.

efforts to sound positive. Men are often more fragile than they appear, and she stays alert to ward off Marie and Linda "ganging up" on Robert.

All of them are dealing with significant change, which is never isolated. Major life events impact people beyond the person experiencing change, and the closer you are to that person, the stronger the ripple effect. Those ripples often become crashing, foaming-at-the-mouth waves. While talking to Marie and Robert the past few days, Angie has encountered a raucous surf and has begun to worry about her future. *What if Robert and Marie need to move away so he can get a good job? What if they need to downsize? I don't have the money to help them, and as I get older, I'll need help too.* She fusses with the dishes and kitchen towels while pretending not to hear the anxious background conversation.

Linda works in strategic planning with her company's executives and has keen insight into traditional business practices. She shares with Robert the outside business pressures that regularly require leadership to course correct for the survival of the company or to leverage opportunities for future growth. Business moves at light speed in this economy, and you don't always see change coming or know why it is taking place. Robert listens, but before long, his eyes glaze over.

"I know it's hard, Rob," Linda says. "But it's time to get an objective, professional opinion. Time to discuss your options with someone who's not your sister-in-law. You should speak with Jennifer."

"I told you I met her for a quick coffee," Marie says. "We didn't talk about money or any kind of financial planning. We talked about life. She's nice. Linda's right. We should go. Up to now, all our decisions have been driven by your old income. If you're not going to replace it, then we need to make a new plan. I need help. We need help."

Early the next week, Robert and Marie tentatively walk into Jennifer's spic-and-span office with comfortable, softly lit seating areas. After a short wait, Jennifer heads their way and welcomes them to an office appointed with a varnished wood table and plush seating. Just as Marie remembers, Jennifer is friendly and kind. Since Marie already met with Jennifer, she sits back, hoping Rob will open up.

"I had a nice coffee with Marie, so I know there's a lot going on in your lives, and I've heard her take but not yours," Jennifer says. "How are you doing, Rob? Anything in particular keeping you up at night?"

"'Keeping me up at night' is the right question," Rob says. "I don't know if I'm tired because I'm confused or confused because I'm tired or angry because I'm confused or confused because I'm angry. All I know is I'm tired of being confused and angry."

"That's understandable," Jennifer says.

"I guess I'm worried about money, that I'll never make that much again. And I can't bring myself to think about what that means down the road."

Jennifer listens, occasionally taking notes, asking smart, appropriate questions in such a way that Robert doesn't feel interrogated. Robert is comfortable with Jennifer and ready to share his concerns and fears and thoughts about his and Marie's future, financially and personally.

"If I'm understanding both of you correctly," Jennifer says, "it sounds like you, Marie, are afraid to spend any money because you only have Rob's temporary severance to count on. And Rob, you just want a job. You don't know if you should sell your house or downsize, cash in your retirement accounts and pay off your mortgage, or maybe cancel or cash in your life insurance policies. It's normal to be nervous about running out of money. Losing a good-paying job at this stage in life is a big deal with many moving parts and layers. Sounds like both of you realize there's a lot to think about and do. Do I understand you correctly?"

"That sums it up," Marie says.

Rob agrees. "In a nutshell."

Jennifer nods. "How about we do this in steps? We could start with what you have, see what resources are available right now before considering what might be your next move. How does that sound?"

Jennifer lists all of their income sources and shows how they can access cash without penalties or substantial taxes. Robert has eight months of severance left and likely unemployment income, and their savings accounts can carry them for many months after. Seeing this information on paper helps them relax; Robert needs a job, but it's not as urgent as they thought, and it won't be rice and beans for dinner every day after all.

They need approximately 75 percent of Robert's prior income to maintain their current lifestyle, and that confirms the fact he needs to work at least a few more years before retiring. He knows he won't be able to replace his income, and it's a tough pill to swallow, but with Jennifer's help, Marie is regaining her identity as the person who can figure it out and make things work. Can she do it? Life isn't all roses for her right now, either; she clearly remembers 2007 to 2009 and shudders to think about that happening again.

"The truth is you've both been successful rising to meet the challenges of your future up to now. And that shouldn't change as you face this 'new' future either," Jennifer says. "Listen, everything in life, your whole world, can and sometimes does dramatically change in the blink of an eye. Market indexes can plunge forty to fifty percent. It's happened before and could happen again and would be catastrophic if you're not prepared. Given the uncertainty and the anxiety that goes along with it, I suggest a process called PMO—purpose, method, outcome—to help you, Rob, better understand what really matters, the why of it, during significant life transitions. Working a few more years isn't your only issue. You miss your old job, the friends you had there, the challenges you faced and overcame every day. Those things helped define you. What I'm suggesting is it's time for you to redefine you."

Right now, Robert's purpose is financial security, the method is a new job, and the outcome is income. Specifically, it's the same or almost the same level of income he previously earned. Jennifer's challenge—or the challenge of any planner presented with this situation—is to present an alternative path to financial security that doesn't require replacing 100 percent of the former income. In this case, Jennifer suggests that perhaps Rob could replicate what he liked best about his previous job experience instead of stressing about every penny.

Income and expenses don't need to balance precisely in the short term; fortunately, Robert and Marie have breathing room before they have to consider a more severe disruption—like selling the house. They can be creative about lowering expenses instead of just cutting things out entirely. Why not do the same things with a different twist? Turn your traditional six-day family vacation into four days, travel closer to home instead of abroad, or consider a good old-fashioned road trip.

Robert nods absently, but then Jennifer says something that gets both his and Marie's attention.

"If you worked outside the home, Marie, it could be the final component that keeps you on financial track."

Marie's hesitation in responding is not uncommon—in similar scenarios, one spouse might not suggest going to work because they hope everything is okay, and the other doesn't want to create more fear. The subject can drum up contention in a relationship, or far worse.

To wit, Robert certainly never even thought about Marie getting a job, and she thought earning $30,000 to $40,000 a year would hardly make a difference. While that might have been true when Robert was bringing home a big paycheck, $30,000 sounds like riches today. After all, they need the money, and being in a lower tax bracket means they keep more of it. If Marie works and can replace 25 percent of Robert's income, he only needs 50 percent of his previous income to get them to Jennifer's suggested benchmark of 75 percent.

Marie imagines all sorts of possibilities, and for the first time in months, she sees a faint light of hope. *If I could work, what would I do?*

In Robert's corner his tunnel vision has been all about making money, but now he realizes he'd be okay with a lower salary in a fulfilling job that works for them. A world with a new and intriguing horizon begins to take shape.

On the drive home from Jennifer's office, Robert and Marie are quiet for a long time, thinking about their meeting, about their future.

Finally Robert nods with some sense of acceptance, feeling better about things. "The floodgates just kind of opened in there."

"That's a good thing," Marie says.

"I feel like I did most of the talking, even though you know much more about our finances. Did I talk too much?"

She reaches over, gently puts her hand on his arm. "You did great, Rob."

THE SISTERS EMBRACE CHANGE

Everything changes again when Marie goes grocery shopping. Looking over the tomatoes and zucchini in the produce aisle, she runs into an old friend, and they catch up with some friendly banter. It turns out the assistant office manager just left her friend's company and there's an opening. Marie's wheels immediately start spinning. She wouldn't have even considered it a month ago, but now it sounds intriguing. *I could do that job. I just need to brush up on my tech skills, and the extra money would be a big help for us.*

A week later Marie is hired and training as an office assistant at a local real estate firm. Starting pay is only $30,000, not nearly enough in the long term, but last week she and Robert were both unemployed with a bleak outlook. Now she has a job with steady income, and the light in the tunnel just got a little brighter.

It's her first full-time job in roughly forty years, however, and a significant change in her schedule and identity. Working full-time takes getting used to—she was the stay-home element, and now she's gone every day, leaving less time at home to manage household responsibilities. But she loves her new job. It's invigorating and brings a social influx she hasn't seen in a very long time.

Life's irony in real time: a devastating and traumatic event for Robert has turned out to be a blessing in disguise for Marie. She's working and growing and back into a rhythm, despite her initial misgivings about going back to work. She thought she would miss the nuances and familiarities of running the household, cooking wonderful meals, and generally keeping their world on track.

It's different now; she's okay with the new day-to-day, and cooking elaborate meals can wait for the weekend. You never know how severe or even noticeable a loss will feel because life can be fulfilling (or far more difficult) in ways you never imagined. Something that doesn't bother you today might be a great big thorn in your side six months later.

These are moments when distressing events channel inner strength, when you find out how strong you can be when being strong is the only option. Cancer survivors, for example, tell us they found strength they never dreamed of but was in there—you can go places you never thought you could; sometimes it just takes an unexpected trigger.

Meanwhile, Marie's sister is adjusting to the opposite scenario.

Linda's company offers an attractive retirement package that inspires a simultaneous blend of excitement and apprehension. She worked in HR during the 2007–2009 financial crisis and remembers the palpable environment of fear people had, waiting for an email summons to an unannounced meeting with their supervisor. That typically meant only one thing, and most everyone was scared; their 401(k) values decreased far too much, and they couldn't afford to retire. Linda wondered if that same scenario could be visited on her, whether a bear market might begin a month after she retires. Retirement sounds exciting, but she has to be smart about it; the last thing she wants is to retire early and then regret it.

She has remained diligent by saving money and funneling it into a 401(k), increasing her contributions when the markets were down and taking on extra work to keep afloat with an eye toward retirement. And yet she still harbors a sense of dread. *What if I lose my job?* She remembers being a single mom, when her ex wasn't much help. She hated feeling like that, but she pushed forward. *I can't change the past or control the future, but I can make good decisions today.*

She ponders pros and cons, life at work or retired life, and what it would be like to fly to that island she keeps dreaming about and spending a few weeks with her toes in the sand.

Freedom matters to Linda. She has waited more than twenty years to achieve it. Her path was partly forced when her husband became her ex-husband, but she chose to work hard and raised two wonderful kids. She turned down spa days or shopping trips with her friends, stayed in her lane, and kept working. That limited time, money, and life's little luxuries, and now it's "me" time. Corporate life has been challenging and fulfilling, and that kept her focused. Now she's ready for "free time and free mind" to do things for herself.

A job fills the need for challenging activities with measurable progress.

Many people don't understand or appreciate that value until it's gone.

Linda is also very sharp, and while retiring sounds sublime, she doesn't want to make any wrong moves that would threaten her freedom. Her job means security, income, a respected position, and great relationships. Letting go of a disciplined routine and a busy schedule can be more difficult than it sounds. The good news is that change management is a big part of HR and Linda has facilitated training around the topic for years; she knows it will be challenging.

Two of the biggest hurdles in retirement are finding new routines and finding new relationships. Linda already envisions a community or nonprofit connection in cancer research to continue efforts made by her company, but it has to be flexible. In fact, the more she thinks about her new freedom, the more excited she gets. *What will I do first? What do I need to create? How do I "start" retirement?*

Establishing new routines and relationships is a start, but her rhythm will be disrupted and gaps need to be filled. She's going from structure to freedom, deadlines to flexibility, and priorities to choices.

How wonderful! How frightening! A job fills the need for challenging activities with measurable progress. Many people don't understand or appreciate that value until it's gone.

But Linda is ready. After traditional goodbyes at work and retirement gatherings, she bids adieu to her longtime employer and sails off into the virtual sunset.

Decision time starts straight away, and her first big plan is to sell her home and buy a smaller condo or townhouse that allows the opportunity to realize her dream of traveling. But before diving into those plans, Linda wants to share her retirement and home sale news with her family, and there's no better stage than Robert's sixty-second birthday party.

Sitting in Marie and Robert's "bonus kitchen," Linda pours wine for everyone in preparation for the big announcement.

But Angie abruptly steals the show with a "drop the mic" moment. "I've decided to sell my house and move in with Linda."

Having come out of nowhere, that slams the brakes on Linda's momentum. The attention in the room shifts to Angie. Linda hears conversation among the others, but it sounds faint and far away; she's lost in a new tangle of thoughts. *Now what do I do? Buy a bigger place so Mom has room? I can't afford that. If she pitches in on the cost, it might work. What about the freedom I had in the palm of my hand? Mom will need tending to, and I just can't leave whenever I want to take a trip somewhere. Sigh.*

REACTION TO CHANGE

When the flurry of emotions, questions, and concerns dies down, Linda finally has an opportunity to share her news, and the same scene unfolds. *Congratulations. When did you decide? What are your plans? This is so exciting.*

In an ironic twist, Angie's thoughts take an abrupt turn. She was never worried about Linda retiring; she has looked forward to having more time with her daughter and had a grand plan to move in with Linda. No one else knew of that idea, but it didn't diminish Angie's excitement for another new life chapter. Is it all at risk of changing now? It sounds like Linda wants to travel a great deal, maybe for months at a time, and they haven't been apart like that for decades. How will they keep their close connection?

"Mom, we'll still be able to talk and even see each other. They have apps for that," Linda says.

"You make it sound easy, but I'm only getting older, and my health ... I need to see my children in person, not on a tiny screen," Angie says. "Well, whatever it is, we'll figure it out. The last thing I would do is let my family drift apart."

Angie ends on a positive note, but it's a blow she wasn't expecting. *I guess I won't be living with Linda after all.* She loves Linda's neighborhood—there's a YWCA nearby, it's close to shopping and restaurants, and there are plenty of smooth sidewalks for walking. She was so looking forward to the sidewalks; she doesn't like walking on the streets, with their unexpected drop-offs and cars whizzing by too fast. She has found a church near Linda's home as well, and plenty of medical providers and clinics. She had the five or so years all planned out in her head. Now what?

Instead of moving to an exciting, exhilarating new place, Angie isn't just letting go of spending more time with Linda, she's losing a vision of a whole new life and needs to create a new canvas—what will her future look like? Will it still include plenty of family time? She realizes her opportunities for memorable life experiences are dwindling while her daughters' are increasing. Changes bring uncertainty, of course, and Angie has had enough of that with advancing years and the nuisance of health problems. She counts on her daughters' support and worries that Linda might fall in love with some faraway place and stay there.

Marie echoes her mother's sentiments. Linda is Marie's best friend, they're always there for each other, and they need to stay connected. *We can't lose that, whether Linda is here at home or traveling the world.* Their connection started at home as young kids and is stronger than ever today; they talk nearly every day and get together at least once a week. How will that dynamic change if Linda is traveling so much? Marie hadn't considered how much Linda's retirement would affect their relationship. In fact, she thought they would have even more time together, not less. Most people talk about traveling when they retire. But most don't plan to leave for months at a time. *When Linda travels, we'll almost always be in different time zones. I can't call her whenever I feel like it, she won't stop by just to hang out, and our impromptu sister outings won't happen much anymore. Wow, she hasn't even left on her first trip and I already miss her.*

Marie finds herself in the same space as her mother: she needs to find a way to stay connected with Linda. They will have to get comfortable with using social media or apps to replace personal interactions. It's far from ideal, given what they're used to, but they have to make it work to adjust to this new change. Their time will be limited, plain and simple, so Marie needs to foster other relationships. Fortunately her new daily routine at work has already sown those seeds.

Where does that leave Robert?

He panicked a little as well after hearing Linda's retirement news. He knows Marie and her sister are close and being together makes them happy. He has enjoyed it as well, especially when Linda would come to their house—this was his alone time to putter in the garage or work on projects, go out with the guys or even just take a nap. Now Linda is retiring and plans to travel. Their traditional family time will change; he'll need to spend more time with Marie to take her mind off losing her "Linda time." But then again, Marie is working now, leaving him the proverbial odd man out. He realizes he will miss Linda as well. He never had to put much effort into their time together, but now he's effectively losing two significant relationships in a short period of time and has no idea how to create more family time.

COMPROMISE AND A NEW NORMAL

In the weeks leading up to retirement, Linda worked with her financial planner, Jennifer Rose, to develop a plan with equal parts strategy and peace of mind. She realized downsizing was a requirement for early retirement to work, so she looked at smaller townhomes, eventually selecting one with great exterior looks, manageable size, lower utility and insurance costs, lower property taxes, and, best of all, a very affordable price. Maintenance costs would also be much less, and of course she wouldn't have commuting expenses anymore.

But that plan took an abrupt turn when her mother announced plans to move in. Linda struggled with this for a time; she was ready and excited to retire, not take care of Angie day after day, but her mother assured everyone the move was to be closer to her daughters and make the most of her closing years.

Her wishes are not uncommon; many of us choose to spend more time with family than friends as we age, and Linda rides waves of selfishness for making travel plans when her mom only wants as much time as possible with her daughters. It would be a sad scene if Angie were to die or fall very ill while Linda was roaming some faraway country.

So once again, Linda calls Jennifer for help. "The new townhome isn't large enough for me and Mom, but the financial plan we put together says I can't retire early and afford a larger place. What are my options?"

"If you planned on spending two hundred and fifty thousand, but three hundred and twenty-five thousand is more realistic for a home that will comfortably accommodate both you and your mother," Jennifer says, "can you ask her to pitch in on the purchase?"

Linda is intrigued; that might be the answer she's looking for. Angie's financial situation, however, is a mystery, so Linda calls Marie, who is equally in the dark about their mother's money—other than that she owns a debt-free home and has enough income to live comfortably. The sisters reflect on how many times they've asked Angie if she is okay financially and the reply has been "I'm fine. Your father took good care of me." Not satisfied with a vague answer like that, Linda and Marie decide it's time to have a talk with Mom.

At Marie's house, Angie's financial papers on the kitchen counter between them, Linda assesses the situation. "Okay, Mom, you have roughly two hundred thousand dollars in savings and other investments, and you own your house free and clear."

"After a little updating," Marie says, "you should walk away with one hundred and fifty thousand."

"Half of which could go toward the purchase and routine expenses of the new townhouse," Linda says.

"That sounds good," Angie says. "And I can take care of the place while you travel."

Life is nothing if not unpredictable. Plans change, directions turn in ways we don't expect, but things have a way of working out. Angie wanted to move into Linda's current home, but that changed; Linda wanted to downsize, and that changed. Both of their plans, well thought out and exciting (despite Angie's secrecy), were disrupted, and excitement turned to worry. But they talked it through and reached an agreeable compromise that benefits them both.

With a new spring in her step, Linda calls Jennifer with her decision to spend an additional $75,000 for a townhome with enough room for Angie. There are limitations on "gifting" money to children, and since she doesn't have Angie's financial details, Jennifer suggests they talk with Linda's CPA for further guidance and then sit down for a meeting.

Linda cringes—her mother abhors talking about money—but Jennifer shares many reasons to include a trusted family member in important family decisions. Children often rightly assume their aging parents don't want to talk about money issues, but in fact, parents typically want someone in the family to be familiar with financial details and ensure sound decisions are made. Far too many seniors are victims of fraud and identity theft, and Jennifer is confident Angie will be relieved to have her daughters more involved.

There are lots of questions to answer, such as those around estate planning, before another meeting with the financial planner and a CPA. The sisters put their collective skills to work and arrange the next sit-down strategy. At the meeting, big-picture details funnel into an action plan that ushers in a new, whole-family life episode, introduced by Linda's long-anticipated wanderlust.

TRAVELS AND TRAVAILS

By midway through the year, Linda has piled up thousands of miles jetting to places on her travel wish list and seen things she's dreamed about since childhood. She savored every minute, but being away from home and familiar surroundings changed her mindset. With plenty of "me" time to think and write a daily journal, Linda has had the opportunity to process the string of significant life events that unfolded in just a six-month flicker.

When life's changes do their thing, life itself isn't the only thing that looks different; our view of the world and who we are also changes.

Linda's journal first revealed where she was—notes on great adventures and how she felt at the time. She was in her "place" and not ashamed to be reveling in every moment—she scored oceanside tables at five-star restaurants, sipped margaritas on tropical beaches, snorkeled with manatees, and ziplined in a jungle. At night she sunk into three-hundred-thread-count dreams. It was cloud nine every day. As time passed, however, the journal entries were less about the latest activities and more about feelings. A shift had begun from living the moment to thinking about tomorrow. *What's next? Will my future be as exhilarating as what I have right now? Do I really want that?*

It wasn't that long ago that she couldn't wait for retirement and new places, people, and experiences, with no job-related fires to put out every day. She could wake up excited each morning, carefree, no place to go and all day to get there.

In the past she tended to just work hard and not get too caught up in the what and why of everything going on. While that intensity and stress and structured calendar have faded, she still makes a to-do list (old habit), but it's much different than in "the old days." Today's lists are should-dos or could-dos or wouldn't-it-be-fun-to-dos instead of must-dos. The look of the new list is great, but she notices gaps in her life that weren't there before.

She was the anchor with kids and family, and she fit the role perfectly, but now she needs to create new routines and relationships. Her job also shaped her social world, and that was a saving grace; she simply didn't have time to establish an intentional social life, and now she's out traveling the world, but she's doing it alone, with no team or family to count on or commiserate with when a day gets choppy. Loneliness is not a pleasant experience. She can avoid the feeling of loneliness for a few hours or a day by finding the next must-go five-star restaurant or taking surfing lessons, but the feeling doesn't go away for long.

She has played some impromptu tennis matches at resorts and enjoyed interacting with other people and even made some new friends. Still, she realizes retirement is changing her identity, and journaling has brought clarity to help her see what is really important. She's checked off plenty of items from her bucket list, and it feels great; she wouldn't change a thing. But it's time to go home. She'll have to adjust to a new home and living arrangement, but the pull is there all the same.

The rest of her life awaits, and she starts to see it in a different light. Her responsibilities have dramatically changed, but the initial shock is less severe; she was worried about her mom moving in, but Marie and Robert stepped in to spend more time with Angie when needed, even when she said, "Don't worry about me; I'm fine. You have enough in your own life to worry about."

The scenario has improved over time. Linda and Marie have kept in touch a few times a week, and knowing Angie is involved with a local church and senior center has lifted Linda's spirits.

Angie is a firecracker and exuberant life participant. She volunteers at the senior center, signs up for classes and activities, and walks regularly with new neighborhood friends. That frees Linda from so much worry and allows her the opportunity to slow down and reflect.

While she genuinely identified with the nomad life, six months of living out of a suitcase in strange places got old. You can't attack and overcome flight delays and botched hotel reservations; you just endure, manage the stress, and trust things will work out. At the same time, a fix isn't always necessary; sometimes the solution is to relax and enjoy the moment. Her traveling "problems" certainly weren't the same as handling challenges at work. Instead of tangible satisfaction or even a mini celebration, it's just take-a-deep-breath relief that the disruption is over.

She's not complaining, but while the freedom of retirement is great, travel and leisure aren't as fulfilling as she expected. She has missed family and friends and, ironically, having structure and routine. Living the "beach" life was such a stark contrast to her past life. Vacations are great escapes from the daily grind of emails, parades of meetings, and deadlines. Linda always loved breaking free from that slog; getting away and unplugging was euphoric in a sense. One of her favorite things to do was leave an out of office email message: *I will be out of the office and TOTALLY unplugged for the next seven days.* But when she retired, she unplugged from work for good, and traveling didn't have the same effect. When the work grind isn't there at all, vacations aren't much of a contrast. Eventually, traveling becomes the grind.

> Transitions don't play fair. They can be and often are messy, and there's no way to anticipate how you will feel or think.

Her journal reflects this disparity: *Is there a difference between a vacation and traveling? When I was working, traveling really felt like a vacation. Now traveling feels like ... traveling. It's wonderful but doesn't feel like a vacation. It's different from my daily life, but I thought I'd be much happier. The contrast to traditional daily life makes vacationing so wonderful; remove the intensity of work and the need to relax and unplug is completely different.*

Transitions don't play fair. They can be and often are messy, and there's no way to anticipate how you will feel or think. Things don't always go the way you want or expect; you encounter surprise, doubt, and confusion that you have to work through.

Linda sometimes forgets how much change has affected her life in the past six months. She retired from a longstanding job she enjoyed and left behind good friends. She sold her home, filled with memories floor to ceiling, a place where her children grew up and she became the person she is today. She picked out a new home in a new neighborhood and then learned her mother planned on moving in as well. All of these changes are major life events, and compounding them makes decision-making more challenging.

Life changes take you out of rhythm, making you feel unsettled and anxious about important decisions. Major changes almost always require financial decisions. When life changes, money changes, and when money changes, life changes again. You can create a sound budget and plan one day, and then life throws a curveball and you have to do it all over again. You must be aware that life changes constantly and affects decision-making and that every change inspires uncertainty about the future. It is difficult to make decisions when you have no idea what's going to happen in the next few months or years. Financial planning never ends; you have to adapt it to an evolving life.

Putting the pen down and closing her travel journal for the time being, Linda breathes in deeply a final tropical sunset, content in the decision that tomorrow she will go home.

A NEW BEGINNING

When the last severance check arrives, Robert carries it from the mailbox to the house but doesn't open it right away or even set it on the counter. He wanders onto the deck, clinging to the envelope like a security blanket. He doesn't want to open it; if he does, that last bastion of hope could fade like the evening's sunset. Marie isn't home from work yet, and he drops heavily into a chair and looks up at cloud puffs drifting lazily across a sapphire sky. His thoughts drift as well, to that day he lost his job, his security, and the sense that protecting their income was the only thing that mattered. But time has a way about it, and eventually Robert settled down with new and more realistic expectations. He still doesn't know how they will manage financially and sits there on the deck holding on to a paper talisman of dwindling self-worth, or perhaps a seed of faith.

About the time he reaches the bottom of a second cup of coffee the next morning, the phone rings. Robert's time volunteering and networking has spread his name around, and the manager of a local sales distributor is on the line with a job offer. He accepts the offer and immediately calls Marie with the news.

"That's great, Rob."

"I know. It's just … "

"It's just what?"

"The salary is forty percent less than I was making."

"That was a long time ago now. Like a lifetime or two."

"It's not just the money. It's losing time with you. I'm used to seeing you more, and part of me doesn't want to give that up."

"We'll figure it out. We always do. Meanwhile, it's a huge step forward, and one we desperately needed. Unemployment is over. New job on the horizon. Time to celebrate."

He can't help but smile. "Time to shake off financial stress, get my head back on a positive track, and move forward with purpose."

"We'll do it together."

"We always do."

Life is changing for Robert and Marie again in big ways that will shape their tomorrow. Robert's travel initially feels like a negative, but they will learn to be more intentional with their time together. Many people go through the same thing and endure much more difficult situations and do just fine. Robert's perspective turns a full and robust 180 degrees; they are at a pivot point of life-changing personal growth. *We're going to be okay.*

Across town, in her new townhome with her new roommate, Linda is feeling the same thing: *We're going to be okay.*

She has thought through some of these big life events, but the decision-making process today is different from the one a year or two ago. Now that she's in the thick of it, everything has changed. Financial decisions in particular take on new trajectories—life changes, and what you wanted in the past doesn't hold the same value anymore. She will need to revisit some of these choices to determine what is still possible and what is still important.

Two of her priorities just walked through the front door—Danny and Justin, ages thirty-four and thirty-one, respectively. Danny is an engineer in the city. Justin teaches history at the university. They both live within a three-hour drive and have decided to surprise Mom together.

Linda is incredibly proud of her boys, and a mini family reunion was just what she needed. Her sons are excited to hear about her wonderful adventures, but in a surprise to Linda, they ask more about what it's like to have all that freedom. They are fascinated to hear what it feels like to have no impediments to anything you want to do, to just pick up and spend half a year traveling to exotic places and seeing the world.

It's an interesting conversation for Linda. She has felt a bit of the been-there-done-that syndrome with a blank day planner and freedom to do whatever she wanted, and now she wants a little routine back in her life. Of course, the kids don't understand; they're still young and think endless freedom is surely life's nirvana, but they haven't experienced it.

The FIRE (financially independent, retire early) movement is popular with young people, and Danny and Justin dream about it too. What they see as the ultimate aphrodisiac isn't that riveting to Linda; life without a routine, consistent relationships, and challenging activities isn't fulfilling. She can't fault her children for thinking the way they do. At their ages, she thought the same way. Life was hard, and work was intense. But it was fulfilling, even more so than she realized at the time.

Moving to a new home and traveling was tiring, but she knows she'll get over it and that it will likely take another year to get comfortable with her new life. *I thought this would be a breeze, but it's going to take time.*

REIMAGINE. REBOOT. REINVENT.

The Passage stage of transition is exciting, challenging, and a time to embrace a new life chapter. Many people want to rush through it and, in effect, get back to the status quo. For all intents and purposes, you've lost your previous identity. You are morphing into a new person through a haze of fatigue and confusion in the midst of inconsistency and change. As Passage begins, you mostly think of the past and what you lost. Thinking about the future comes later. Initially, you feel unsettled and miss your old routine.

Halfway through this stage, however, your focus begins to shift. You feel energized and start to reimagine what life could be like instead of lamenting what you lost (which you never get

Remember that life events are neutral until we assign a value— negative or positive, window closed or door opened. A life event doesn't need to be viewed as a good thing to be a growth thing.

back anyway). You can feel it. It's time to reboot and create a new life and a better version of you. Traumatic events leave scars, and you'll never forget what has happened, but that doesn't mean you can't lean in, move forward, and grow as a person. At this halfway point, you see glimpses of a possible future. It's more like a sketch than a clear picture, but it's something, and the seeds of hope take root.

Remember that life events are neutral until we assign a value—negative or positive, window closed or door opened. A life event doesn't need to be viewed as a good thing to be a growth thing. All life events, from wonderful blessings to traumatic losses, can lead to personal growth over time. This halfway point during Passage is critical. Growth accelerates when your thoughts and actions become more intentional. Meaning, you respond in a thoughtful manner rather than with knee-jerk reactions. Your decisions today become more influenced by what you want tomorrow.

Now you're ready to shape your future.

Unfortunately, a switch doesn't flip in your brain to signal the midpoint of Passage. This transition stage is the longest and doesn't end quickly. Sure, you can adapt rapidly to minor changes, like a new position at work, but major life events like losing a job or divorce can take years to work through. It's not as simple as saying, "I'm fine and moving on."

Interestingly, the same type of fight or flight advice Robert received when he lost his job applies here. Well-intentioned but conflicting advice pours in seemingly from all directions: In the morning, your type-A friend says, "Hey, you've got to get back up on the horse; come on, you got to make something happen. What's your plan for today?"

Later that day, a more thoughtful friend says, "Take a step back and take care of yourself; life is overwhelming sometimes. Why don't you join me in my restorative yoga class?"

And then those bighearted, well-meaning people want to help even more and regale you with their own story of being overwhelmed. Suddenly it's not about you anymore. *Maybe he'll feel better if I tell him about a similar experience that ended well.* "Hey, Robert, I went through something similar, and I know how you feel." Or, "I have a friend who went through this and had a better job ninety days later." All the while, Robert thinks to himself, *It's similar but not the same. You don't know how I feel. Even worse, I also have a friend who went through this, and he's still unemployed.* It's great that family and friends want to help, and you need support, but it can be too much, quickly become overwhelming, and end up making you feel worse.

A LIFE EMBRACE

Marie can't wait to go to work. She never imagined having a morning routine like this as part of her life, much less enjoying it. In an unexpected twist, she realized working outside of the home suits her, not just for the money but also for genuine personal satisfaction. She smiles inside on the drive to the office and looks forward to what the day might bring. There's always a new challenge, her coworkers are ambitious and vibrant, and she is thriving in an environment that rewards attitude and effort.

The person who last had this job left things in disarray, and Marie was told as much when she started. But she's a born fixer. She approaches tasks with intention and figures things out. Her coworkers' expectations were low due to past events, and they are continually surprised and impressed at her ability to accomplish projects quickly and accurately. Learning her position and the nuances of the real estate business is challenging, but she enjoys the new social relationships, and setting, tracking, and meeting regular goals is energizing.

Marie forgot how fulfilling work could be, and it's great to feel competent and necessary in different ways than she had become used to. She has always been the "figure things out" person, and the new job allows that spirit to shine every day. Humans are wired to be productive. It's what we do, and it sometimes goes against the perspective of working hard in a career, then retiring, and sitting back on the front porch. Reality, however, looks different. People who do very little in their retirement years generally don't have a high quality of life; their health suffers, and many have shorter lifespans. On the other hand, active and productive people thrive, and there are many ways to do that.

Marie did it. She led a stay-at-home life for many years and built a life she enjoyed, but it's different than being challenged in the workplace and developing relationships in that kind of environment. That's not to say one is better or worse than the other, but many retired people say their working years were the best of their lives, and Marie is realizing that in real time. She's far more than just okay with her new job; she loves it and feels alive and energized.

Her social relationships have changed as well. When you're in a nonwork, stay-at-home environment, friends and other social relationships can be more as-needed support. When you're struggling with something or going through a big life transition, your friends are there for you, yes, but most nonwork, stay-at-home days don't bring significant struggles or challenges that require their support.

The level of engagement and fulfillment in a social network at her work is different; most people are actively engaged in helping their coworkers succeed and coming together to figure things out. Nobody appears to be counting down the days to when they can get Social Security and finally retire. There's a different intensity level when people are trying to thrive, not just survive. At the end of the day, it's good to be needed.

Marie spent so much time thinking about money in the past. Robert made X amount of money and would only work X number of years. There was no money tree in the backyard. Eventually, Robert would retire, and they would rely on Social Security and their retirement savings. She needed to pinch pennies when she could and not put too much stress on Robert. Then he lost his job and the paychecks ended. Just like that, the budget didn't work. Her lifelong anxieties over money turned to fear. It didn't matter how long she stared at her spreadsheet and massaged the numbers. The bottom of the column was red, and she couldn't cut enough to balance the columns. Those memories are both recent and vivid. She *never* wants to feel that way again.

Now Marie isn't focused so much on their household bottom line. Instead, she's looking more at the top line and the increasingly clear picture that this new scenario could be even better. She starts to think about money differently—*Next year I'll make even more money, and I really enjoy the work*—and there is a significant pendulum swing in how she and Robert view spending and saving. Marie was used to working solely with the money Robert made and stretching it to cover their lifestyle, but now she has choices and something previously unfamiliar: the opportunity to invest in herself. She never needed to do that before or felt the impulse to do so, instead of saving every penny and living frugally. Today she is in a place of growth, and while her office position requires a degree of decorum and appearance she's not used to, she revels in the excitement of it all.

At a late dinner on their deck, Marie and Robert talk about money. But now, in light of their transitions, they seem to have traded points of view.

"I'm not worried about it, Rob. And I don't think you should be. I mean, I don't want you to be worried about it either. You never used to. I was always the worrier."

"I know; it's just still a little hard to swallow. Forty percent is a big drop. I can't save like I used to. So I'm asking myself if we'll really be okay."

"And I'm telling you we will. Nothing in life is guaranteed. But I can work and make money for the foreseeable future, and now so can you. We don't need to withdraw anything from the nest egg. That's great. I feel better about our budget than I have in years, maybe ever."

He's thrilled for her, of course. But he knows her better than anyone. "So what's the hitch? I feel a hitch. Is there a hitch hiding in there somewhere?"

She smiles. She loves that he knows her better than anyone. "There is. The hitch is that staying active, eating right, getting enough sleep, and other 'normal' parts of what used to be my 'normal' day are harder with a full-time job. There are only so many hours to get it all done. Free time is at a premium now. I have to be more intentional about taking care of myself."

He laughs out loud. "Me too."

She still loves the sound of his laugh, and it's been a while since she's heard it. "Yes, you too."

Within just a few months, the office is buzzing, and the agents push for Marie to hire someone for part-time admin help. They see how valuable Marie is and want her to hand off some routine tasks. Marie is a problem-solver, so they want her to have more time to figure things out. And just like that, Marie is a manager, with a subsequent income boost.

"Ask Marie; she'll figure it out" is a common refrain around the office. She smiles when she hears it and thinks to herself, *Yes, I will.*

That's what I do. Working with a team to manage and solve problems is stimulating and fulfilling, and she discovers capabilities she never thought she had. In fact, Marie has referred a couple of friends to the real estate agency, and they have both completed transactions; this inspires thoughts of getting licensed and sharing in commissions. She sees potential for even more income by listing and selling properties. She's not enamored with the idea of shifting to straight commission, but participating more in the sales process is enticing.

On her way home from work, Marie reflects on life's fascinating, frustrating, joyous moments and feels a new kind of peace. Robert is enjoying his new job as well, they've adjusted to spending time together on weekends, and all is right with the world. She looks forward to sharing her new sales potential at work with the rest of the family and hopes they are in as fine a place.

CROSSROADS

Linda is home but feels unsettled. After Robert's sixty-third birthday, the traditional family talk session was enjoyable as always, but she felt hazy, and the others' voices sounded muffled. Life felt immediately different when she returned from traveling, but she can't figure out why. Retiring, moving into a new home, and moving her mom in didn't leave much time to establish new routines. She understands that life has changed but didn't think she would feel this "off." She took off on her travels so quickly there wasn't time to create, or even really consider, her new, postwork life—what does she do now?

She remembers a previous conversation with Jennifer, her financial planner, about how retiring changes your perspective on money. She stayed on budget and is still "on track" with various accounts, but today it hits her like a heavyweight left hook: *This is it. My nest egg is all I have, and I'm not saving and adding to it anymore. Even worse, I'm taking from it. I didn't need this money before and didn't think about it much back then. Now I retired early, and what I see is all I have. I should have saved more. Is this really enough? What if Mom needs help? What about my kids? They're fine now, but you never know.*

Jennifer explained some other unexpected retirement nuances, such as watching financial news more often and checking account balances every other day. It can be unsettling, scary, and even nauseating at times. Years of savings can seem to disappear overnight. Money that was meant to fulfill your dreams vanishes, or at least that's how it feels sometimes.

Linda's life has changed significantly over the past several years, so becoming more concerned about money is normal. Understanding why she feels different is the key to putting her fears in perspective. Jennifer helps ease her angst and see the contrast between today and a few years ago.

"It's normal to need some time to fully absorb everything that's happened," Jennifer says. "There's a whole range of feelings people experience when they finally retire. Think about it. You were employed and earning a comfortable income. Now there's no longer a regular paycheck, bonuses, or annual raises."

Linda nods. "Check, check, and check."

"Plus, you moved from the home where you raised your children and created the memories of a lifetime. Now you're in a townhome with your mother."

"I love my townhome and my mother, but still … " Linda's voice trails off.

"But you're no longer adding funds to your 401(k) and savings account. You've switched from investing and saving to withdrawing and spending. You went from salary to no salary. Multiple changes have a compounding effect. With that many changes, some people may feel anxious or overwhelmed, while others might feel depleted or angry. And then some people absorb it quickly, feel energized, and are ready to move forward. Everyone is different. How are you feeling with all of this?"

Linda is much more in tune with the latest financial news, but speaking with Jennifer sheds light on what apparently is becoming her new normal. Becoming more concerned about the economy and the markets is a common occurrence in the world of retirees, but Linda is a rookie. It's not like she has retired ten times before. This is new territory for her. Jennifer validates the anxiety and confirms that, yes, the next recession or bear market could take hold any day. However, it's essential to be aware of the media's traditional plan of attack.

Many newscasts and websites frequently predict recessions and bear markets. Those events happened in the past, so we can expect the same to happen again in the future. Eventually, the financial soothsayers will be right. Of course, the question is when, and answering it carries the same accuracy as predicting the weather on a Tuesday six months from today.

Jennifer reminds Linda that the media have two goals—attraction and action—and neither is meant to help you. It's no secret that they sensationalize facts and play on people's emotions. Headlines attract attention, and that means page views and money from advertisers. Their goal is to keep you watching or reading (that's the action part). Jennifer suggests thinking of it as content versus delivery—the problem isn't necessarily the content conveyed; it's the delivery method. Stories are sensationalized, and the media loves to talk about how bad things can get. The challenge is to be aware and stay informed but not watch the news 24-7.

It makes sense, but Linda is still uneasy. *Should I know more about these things than I did before? Should I just trust my planner and try not to worry? I know of people who trusted some financial person and lost money.*

Over the next weeks, she gradually develops a system and replaces worry with exercise and social interaction. A local pickleball club hosted an event over the weekend, and she got in on a few lively games, feeling kind of like a kid again with an energy she hasn't had since those first days of free-spirited traveling.

There is a direct connection between being active and reducing stress in favor of happiness, and Linda is living it in real time. It doesn't take long, and she becomes one of the club's newest members.

Interestingly, being part of this group of people is the spark Linda needed. Now she plays pickleball regularly and loves the mostly friendly competitiveness, challenging herself to improve, and makes new friends nearly every time with her kind of people—involved in the community, active, intentional about doing things that bring value to their lives. Linda was always too busy in the past to be involved much in the community, but new relationships and activities have her head in the clouds. Could it get any better?

OPPORTUNITY KNOCKS

Energized after a midweek pickleball match, Linda meets a pair of gregarious women, and soon they are huddled around a courtside bistro table. It turns out the ladies are running a small catering business, which at the moment is plagued with a staffing issue. Linda lived human resources for years and offers a few ideas.

Her new friends beam. "Are you a consultant? How do you know about all this? Are you available to help us?"

Linda is glad to and after a couple of meetings at the catering shop, agrees to help in a more formal capacity, smoothing the staffing-related waters. Something clicks. Linda realizes she misses the high of overcoming challenges and figuring things out. Even better, she's helping her friends succeed and move forward, and it's energizing for everyone.

"You're so good at this. I wish you'd been around when we started," one says.

"You could be a business consultant," the other adds.

Maybe I could, Linda thinks. *Maybe I should. I really enjoy helping my friends and their company. Is there an opportunity here? What would it look like if I worked a few days a week, or just one project at a time?*

The club community helps make the decision. Word spreads faster than in a high school rumor mill that Linda knows how to get things done, and soon all kinds of people invite her to help out at charities and with other business ventures. Linda begins to reimagine retirement. She accepts a few consulting offers and enjoys helping nonprofits but doesn't see it as a regular gig.

People grow and change, especially after major life events. It's hard to know who you'll be and what you'll want farther down life's road. Over time, priorities may shift, and we may think and feel differently about many things. Predicting the future is even more challenging than planning for the future. It's the way life works. We mature and become different people. Linda's entire family illustrates this to a T, and they discuss it with verve at the annual birthday party reflection get-together—Robert's sixty-fourth birthday.

Linda didn't know she would feel how she does today.

Marie had no idea she'd fit in so well at her new job and establish a rewarding career.

Robert certainly didn't expect to completely shift gears and start a new job.

We all have values and various things that are important to us, and many of those remain with us for life. There's no way to know the extent that life changes will impact us intuitively.

For example, you might enjoy and thrive in the outdoors and purposely live in a place that fosters that lifestyle. But it doesn't mean your dream retirement must be in Colorado or New Mexico or Morocco. One aspect of life is just that, one aspect. The essence is what matters. There are many ways to put together a puzzle, but if you're too prescriptive about it, you miss a lot of other possibilities.

> *There's no way to know the extent that life changes will impact us intuitively.*

It's essential to anchor on what's important but leave yourself open to other opportunities. And this goes against Linda's past experiences. She always had specific goals and people and corporate departments, but now she has freedom. It's an exciting new way of thinking, so why is she still on edge?

CAREER 2.0

Linda floats a bit, working for nonprofits, volunteering here and there, playing pickleball, and it's all under a lingering, pesky dark cloud. Volunteering isn't overly stressful or challenging, and for her that means it's unfulfilling. It's great to be busy, but it's not the same as being productive with something you enjoy; there's a marked difference, and she feels it. She recalls a conversation with Jennifer focused on how high-achieving personalities often struggle during retirement. On retirement day they may say, "That's it. I'm finished working," and six months later they're in a part-time job or consulting in their industry. It happens all the time.

A retirement nomad life may sound wonderful, but it doesn't check all the boxes that make a fulfilling life, and many people circle back to some kind of work. Linda is now doing the same thing. She couldn't wait to retire and travel, and now she's consulting with her club's members, but things have changed again; it's time to get back to work. Not the fifty-hour-week kind of work, but work that matters. Now there are decisions to make.

Should she form an independent consulting company or buy into her friends' catering business? She knows virtually nothing about starting and running a business, and while working twenty or thirty hours a week seems okay now, how long will it hold her interest? Not that long ago, she had no interest in working, didn't even think about it early on in her travels. Then she started to think differently. Now she knows she needs to work or do something! For how long? It doesn't matter. She just knows right now she's not fulfilled.

More important than an endpoint is making a difference in people's lives and being productive. After an afternoon of pickleball and consulting at the club, Linda sees a text message from her sister. "Come on over for wine on the deck" is music to Linda's ears. She needs to share concerns and relax and laugh. How she missed that when she was traveling.

Linda arrives, and while cradling delicate glass stems as late afternoon sunlight swirls with the ember-red tonic, Marie wastes no time encouraging Linda to run with that energy.

"This is what you do, Lin. You're good at it, and you enjoy it. Start consulting more formally. Buy into that business. Do something. You'll be much happier working even part-time. Look at how it changed me. I'm much more mentally energized than when I stayed at home. I still can't believe I was out of the workforce for so long. I wonder how life would have played out if I had started working sooner."

"I wonder how it would have played out if I'd never stopped."

"Aren't some of your friends still working?"

"Yes. Because they want to be. It makes them happy."

"Sorry to be the one to break it to you, but you're not built to stay at home. My sister the homemaker? Please. I don't see it."

The sisters are laughing like teenagers and Linda's only been here five minutes. *It's so good to be home*, she thinks.

Linda agrees with Marie. She has seen her sister's evolution unfold and wonders, *Could the same thing happen for me?* She doesn't really need extra money, but having an income again would be nice, and a routine with new social relationships sounds wonderful.

Linda shares details from her meetings with Jennifer, and Marie is supportive and intrigued. Jennifer brought up several "what-if" scenarios, including the possibility of Angie needing additional and expensive healthcare.

We obviously can't plan for every "what-if" in life, but preparing always trumps scrambling to fix mistakes or catch up. Because she's been trained to understand both sides of the retirement coin—human and financial—Jennifer also mentioned the importance of rhythm. Life is most fulfilling when you have a routine, are social and engaging in challenging activities, and have ways to measure success.

While Linda generally understood the concept of rhythm when Jennifer first explained it, she now realizes it's necessary, especially at this point in her life. It's time to decide which path to take, but nothing is entirely black and white.

She has reassessed her view on traveling and the other freedoms that came with retirement and concluded that, ultimately, a lot of it is about risks versus rewards.

Every risk, every choice, comes with its own responsibilities and life impact. Is a sense of community service the priority, or is working with a team again in an office sitting at the top of the list? Is it helping people build toward their dreams—her catering business friends, for instance? And what does Linda get out of that? A paycheck is never enough; she knows that. Will the work matter?

Life transitions are rarely simple and straightforward. An event such as retirement has multiple layers of change. Understanding the scope and significance of the different aspects is just not something you can see clearly at first. Changes aren't isolated. When your work routine changes, it impacts your relationships, health, finances, and much more. Linda's journaling helped her process everything that was going on. *This retirement thing is way more intense than I thought.*

Linda has recently experienced the giddiness of travel and early stages of retirement, stress and outright fear of financial uncertainty, an unexpected roommate, and prospects of a new business venture. While she's no stranger to change, it's always challenging in emotional and physical iterations.

Distress is a common byproduct of prolonged and unpleasant change, but *eustress* is also possible. That is a type of stress that's also beneficial and inspires growth. Ultimately, we want to reach a space of physical and emotional stability in which we can make wise and balanced decisions. Even welcome transitions can make your world a little shaky, but working through transition leads to a new, reinvented life. Linda's transition embodies some of the common transition mindsets:

Roller coaster—along for the ride with a white-knuckle grip through terrifying turns and precipitous drops

Tingling anticipation—you know something special is about to happen, and you can hardly contain yourself

Walk in a fog—nothing is clear, and it's difficult to see even a step ahead

Cocoon—you're withdrawn and can't face life

Sunset stroll—everything's roses, and you're savoring the life of your dreams

Right now, however, Linda's primary concern is consistently withdrawing from her nest egg to invest in the catering business. Naturally, she can't keep taking out money. Her plan was tight to begin with. Additional withdrawals are risky. What if disaster strikes and the business closes its doors? Her current portfolio value might not be enough and she could struggle even more to provide what she needs in the clutches of a sudden market decline. Still, Linda understands the risks and is excited about joining the catering business. Change is coming, and anticipation paves the way.

GOLDEN YEARS THROUGH A NEW LENS

While her daughters embrace an exhilarating future, Angie tosses out the aging rule book and seizes every moment. She knows she's slowing down physically and mentally but doesn't let that stop her. She has an upbeat, energetic way about her, "arriving" at new stages and experiences, choosing to build a new life and wringing the best from each day. She's still her kids' go-to and always supportive but is careful not to ask for much and detract from their busy lives. It's important to her that they appreciate what they have and enjoy the moment because life changes so quickly. She experienced it in real time—one day you're having coffee with your husband, and the next, you're planning his funeral.

At the time, Marie naturally shared her mother's sadness of losing Dad too early. Since his passing, she has often called to check on her mother. Angie always says the same thing. "Marie, it's okay; don't worry about me. I'm fine. Where do you think you and your sister learned to figure things out? The women in our family have always been tough; life happens, and we adapt and flourish."

To that end, Angie is all about connecting with friends, volunteering, and getting out around town. She knows some people build walls around themselves and let life trickle toward its end. And although it's tempting at times, she doesn't give in. *Old* doesn't mean a foot in the grave, and, in fact, she often feels more energized than she did twenty years ago. She's more familiar every day with this newfangled texting thing and has learned how to use FaceTime to keep in touch with distant friends (Marie and Linda think it's great and chuckle when Angie scolds her phone for not cooperating).

One of Angie's favorite treats is pressing a button on the phone and having an Uber driver magically appear to chauffeur her all over. She fretted about losing the ability to drive and relying on her kids, but rideshare services keep her engaged with the community. Even better, she can buzz into town for a movie or summer festival or all manner of lively activity. The new senior center is a regular destination, and she's one of the "elders" of the group. Ironically, the younger seniors fill her with energy, and the new retirees are constantly chatting about planning trips and sharing the latest photos of their grandchildren. Angie enjoys (and takes solace in) encouraging others to stay active and enjoy life to its very fullest, and she practices it herself every day.

A new routine has her familiar and comfortable with the new neighborhood, exercise groups, church, and the grocery store. She makes regular appearances greeting at church—it's great helping out and meeting new people. Being around all kinds of different folks has opened up new and unexpected ideas. She feels like the proverbial kid in a candy store. *Energized in my eighties*, she says to herself. *Who would've thought?*

TIME WAITS FOR NO ONE'S RETIREMENT

Later in the week, the family will gather for Robert's sixty-fourth birthday party, this time out on the deck. Since she is working full-time, Marie has less time to plan and prepare than she did in the past. *No problem*, she thinks. *I can throw this together in a few days.* But first, she wants to relax for a few minutes. *The last couple of years have really been something …*

Not that long ago, Robert could see the bright, flashing light of retirement, while Marie saw only an occasional glimmer. Now Robert is entrenched in a brand-new job and Marie is working as well (and loving it). Linda has transitioned from nomadic travel back to a comfortable home life and has also tracked back to the work world. Angie was concerned for them all but is far more content today and happy everyone is adjusting to their new lives and doing well. She settles deep into her lounge chair's downy cushions and imagines the next chapter. What will tomorrow bring?

SCENE 4:

A LIFE IN FLUX

In an old Taoist parable, a farmer in ancient China who owned a horse was told by his neighbor, "You are so lucky to have a horse to pull the cart for you."

"Maybe," the farmer replied.

One day the horse broke free from the corral and ran away. "Oh no! What bad luck!" his neighbors cried.

"Maybe," said the farmer.

A week later the horse returned, bringing with it a herd of wild horses, which the farmer and his son maneuvered into the corral. The neighbors walked over to see the horses and exclaimed, "Oh, what good luck. Now you will be rich!"

"Maybe," said the farmer.

Some weeks later the farmer's son was breaking in one of the wild horses when it threw him off, breaking the son's leg. "Oh no! Such bad luck again," his neighbors said.

"Maybe," replied the farmer.

The next day soldiers came and took away all able-bodied young men to fight in the war, but the farmer's son was left behind due to his injury. The neighbors said, "You are so lucky your son did not have to fight in the war."

"Maybe," replied the farmer.

No matter the event, the farmer doesn't view it as good or bad; it just is. The lesson is we never know how something will turn out. It might not seem like it at the time, but catastrophic events (or even minor everyday annoyances) often come with unexpected benefits. And yet many people are reluctant to recognize those silver linings. Remember that life events are neutral and can have positive and/or negative aspects. People then label events, or aspects of events, good, bad, or otherwise. This behavior is called cognitive appraisal and is necessary for growth. It's not necessary to label a life event as a good thing, but it *is* a growth thing, and it's important to realize that no matter what's going on, no matter the grief or loss, we always have the opportunity to grow. Change can be uncomfortable, but it leads to a growth experience, and if we accept that we can't go back and redo or retry, we can move forward and figure it out.

> *It might not seem like it at the time, but catastrophic events (or even minor everyday annoyances) often come with unexpected benefits.*

STRESS AND THE IMPORTANCE OF MINDSET

Either consciously or not, we choose how we will respond to what occurs in our lives. All events are neutral until we assign a value to them. Psychologists call this cognitive appraisal. When we judge an event as negative, our mood, decisions and actions shift accordingly. Just as importantly, a physiological experience is triggered. If we have a mindset that an event is stressful, we trigger the type of response that can be unhealthy absent an actual life-threatening situation. This judging and reacting happens so quickly most people don't even realize it's occurring. But research shows that *if we continue to feed the idea that our situation is stressing us out,* we can compromise our own cognitive and emotional faculties.

And that is the foundation of what makes Marie Marie. She is confident as a rule and always pushes forward in the midst of changes and challenges. Today she is confident for very different reasons and has no thoughts of retiring anytime soon. In fact, she is more energized than ever and proud of her newfound status as a respected business-woman. She's the figure-it-out (FIO) woman. The FIO at home for many years and now in the office. In addition to managing the office and having hired a direct-report operations position, she has sales percolating, and the potential is there to earn around $100,000 this year. She can hardly believe the change in circumstances. *I might make six figures this year! Three years ago Robert lost his job and we had no idea what we'd do. Now look at us.*

Robert is on a similar trajectory. He has done well at his new job this year and sat down with Marie to review the latest numbers with Jennifer Rose, their financial planner.

"We didn't expect it," Robert says, "but we think Marie's income has changed the game again."

"Retirement is on the table for the second time," Marie says.

Jennifer nods. She's had this exact conversation with other clients in similar circumstances. "I hear you loud and clear. But before you make a decision, let's play a quick round of what-if. What if there's a sudden and drastic market decline? What if there's a recession? What if for unknown reasons Marie's income is reduced from one hundred thousand to thirty thousand? What if she has to stop working entirely? All financial planning carries assumptions of how the world stage will unfold. Should any of these what-ifs play out the wrong way, your new grand plan could fall flat."

Robert nods. He's thought about both sides of the retirement coin, the human and the financial. "I hear you, Jennifer. And I think you're right. But at this point in my life, I'm willing to risk retiring sooner."

"I agree with Rob," Marie says. "We're at the point in our lives where we think it's worth the risk. If something disastrous happens, we'll figure it out. Rob and I are survivors. I don't think we knew it before, but we know it now."

When people are uncertain and don't feel in control, they may be more conservative than is typical for them, focusing on protecting what they have. On the other hand, when they're thriving and see income increasing, they may become more aggressive. Some people vacillate between fear and greed; one moment they don't want any risk due to fear, and the next they want to be aggressive as greed takes over.

In Marie's case, she's making great things happen at work and doesn't see that changing anytime soon. Even so, Jennifer stresses the risk of derailment in their future, even if it is only a "small probability."

Robert and Marie share a glance, and it's clear which direction they wish to take. They have both endured a long, stressful road of transition and challenge, and they have a little swagger.

The resilient couple leaves Jennifer's office hand in hand, striding into the day with faith in their wherewithal to mold a rewarding future. Robert reflects inwardly on his volunteering experience and various projects he was part of. In the past he's always had an eye on the next job. Now he's had that "next job" and can afford to retire and refocus on helping out with different organizations. Marie has no doubt her momentum in the real estate arena will only increase.

Across town, Linda's life takes another unexpected but positive turn when she meets someone through the pickleball club. Jacques recently moved to the United States from France, and his life path is similar to Linda's. She certainly didn't see this coming—she wasn't even looking and was always too busy in the past to think about welcoming a new person into her life. She's building a new, semiretired life, and although she chose the single life after divorce to focus on her children, it's nice to have the attention of another again.

Marie hears of this new development from Angie and immediately calls her sister. They are like a couple of high school friends buzzing about a new boy in class. After some traditional inquiries—"Where he's from? Is he tall, dark, and handsome? What does he like to do?"— Marie wants to know more. She's always thinking about finances and can't resist digging for more on this mysterious man.

Marie is half-kidding. But only half. "So does he have money, or is he after yours?"

Linda shrugs off the subject. "I don't know. He's nice and good-looking and seems well enough off."

"I get it, but money is complicated, even at your age—okay, our age—and when one is retired. It's more than just having money or not."

"I promise to put it on a front burner."

"That's fine, but first you have to promise to introduce him to us."

"Yes, that too."

Interestingly, repartnering, or a formal marriage later in life is commonplace in today's world and brings with it all manner of delights and challenges and adjustments. Boomers and Gen Xers tend to repartner in short periods of time, generally less than three years, and they often get mired in all sorts of financial drama.

Not surprisingly their divorce rate is also quite high. In some cases this stems from the woman having more money than the man in the relationship—and this might be the case with Linda. She's done well and is self-sufficient in retirement but might end up with a man who's not in such a stable financial space. She might suddenly be forced to worry about money for two.

Linda already spent a lot of time thinking through the pros and cons of starting a new business, consulting or working part-time, and suddenly there's a new man in her life, and she has to rethink the whole works. Maybe love is in her future, and instead of building a new space around work and structure, she could take a spontaneous trip with her new beau. He has family in France. It would be grand to travel throughout Europe with her own tour guide.

A single additional variable added to your decision process can influence everything and often requires a complete restart. It's important to understand that what matters now may change tomorrow. Some people are content with where they are and what they're good at right now—and that's fine. But next week a switch can flip, and you have to approach things differently. The old way is long gone and simply doesn't work anymore. Ultimately, it all becomes a perfectly natural way of responding to life's changes.

Angie takes changes in stride as well. She has routines with friends and a structure in place but shows more signs of forgetfulness every day. Linda and Marie pitch in to help whenever they can and have bought their mother a giant calendar for her desk to help with reminders of upcoming events and daily tasks—like the church volunteer committee and lunch every Tuesday and keeping up with medications and remembering to exercise and family birthday parties.

At Robert's sixty-fifth, the entire family has settled into new life chapters. Robert and Marie decide to join the same club where Linda plays pickleball and quickly meet new friends. It's a great place for Robert to stay active, and Marie expands her contacts network. Robert feels great with their home dynamic as well. Marie was always there to help him through tough times, and it's special to support her now. He looks forward to getting back into the volunteering groove, helping with different projects and events. Even more importantly, the stability has a positive effect on their kids—they're all doing well, blossoming in the early stages of careers with homes of their own. Linda's kids have followed similar paths, and a big family reunion is planned for next year. Everyone is excited to catch up.

They all agree on how fascinating life can be. It seems like yesterday when Robert lost his job and he and Marie were thrust into a place of unrest and angst. Linda retired and strolled into a season of flip-flops and travel to tropical islands. Angie sold her house, moved in with Linda, and created an entirely new lifestyle.

Now Robert and Marie are on top of the world, filled with excitement for the future.

Linda had an idea of her next chapter for what seemed like a day or two, and now she's unsure what happens next—there's someone new in her world stirring emotions she hasn't experienced for years.

Angie had some tests run at her clinic, and early signs of dementia are surfacing, but she hasn't told anyone yet. *I don't want to worry them. They already have a lot to handle. I'll tell them later. I just want to spend time with everyone and laugh and tell stories to my grandchildren.* She sees a gradual decline in her health but remains upbeat and supportive of her family.

Each of them share "then and now" stories about how far they've come and what contributed to bringing them to this particular point in life. What made the difference? A common thread for all is a string of decisions that came together to drive change. But while Robert and Marie are in a new normal, Angie and Linda have entered the anticipation stage with significant life events on the near horizon.

Soon the conversation turns to Angie. Everyone knows she's getting older and wants to know how she feels and how they can help. In traditional form, Angie deftly sidesteps the attention, changing the subject to seemingly random world events.

"I've been watching the news about something happening in China. There's a new virus that sounds very serious, and people are getting very sick and dying. I'm a little worried about you kids."

"Yes, Mom, we heard that too," Marie replies. "You shouldn't worry about it. Remember Ebola? The mortality rate was over fifty percent, but they got a handle on it. Unless you're planning on visiting the Great Wall next week, I think you'll be fine."

* * *

Life happens, and it never follows the course we expected or hoped for or planned. It is always in flux, a moving sea of everyday joys, career accomplishments and challenges, growing up, settling down and raising a family, and endless waves of the unexpected. It's certainly possible to tread water, ride wherever life brings us, and hope to stay afloat. But to wring the most from every day and succeed in whatever capacity we choose, we must become captains of this life ship and navigate waters stormy and smooth with a keen eye toward the desired destination.

What is your endpoint or evolving goal? You might have a definitive place all picked out or no idea at all, simply hoping for the best. Whatever the scenario, transitions are the lens through which we shape change into a favorable and enriching form. "Significant life events"—retirement, home purchase, getting a job, losing a job, becoming a parent—have an enormous influence on your approach to the management and outcomes of such transitions.

Change is one constant you can depend on. Embrace it, shape it, and make life your happiness project.

TEN TRANSITION TAKEAWAYS

1. **We can't always control change, but we can shape it.** No matter how exciting or traumatic a life event is, you have the power to shape the transition and grow. Focus on responding thoughtfully instead of reacting emotionally. Change around us fuels change within us.

2. **Financial changes impact life, and life changes impact finances.** Think of life as the human part and money as the financial. Consider both when making financial planning decisions, as there is no such thing as a purely financial decision. Always consider what you are thinking and how you feel when trying to make decisions.

    *   Linda viewed her money differently as soon as she retired. Her net worth was the same, but now she felt differently. For years she saved for tomorrow, hoping to have more money in the future. Once she retired, tomorrow became today. Now there was no more saving from a regular paycheck. She felt like her nest egg, which had grown over the years, had finally hatched. Was it enough? She was confident before, but when life changed, she started having doubts.

3. **Significant events mean big decisions.** Life's most important financial decisions are often required during major life events. When life changes dramatically, you may find yourself in unknown waters asking, *Now what?* Discovering that answer has lifelong implications. The stress and uncertainty make it harder to think clearly in those situations. This is a primary challenge of major life events: the most impactful decisions in life are required when it's hard to make decisions. Remember to slow down and focus on now before worrying about what's next. See the Decision-Free Zone to organize what needs to be done now, soon, or put off until later.

   • Fortunately, Robert and Marie took their time making decisions. They avoided major, regrettable decisions that couldn't be undone.

4. **Guard against complacency.** Life happens, and eventually, plans disrupt. Don't let a season of comfort lull you into thinking this is how life will be for the foreseeable future. When planning, consider what-if scenarios and plan as best you can.

   • If your job and income ended today, what would you do tomorrow? It can happen to anyone. Your position may become redundant, and your job eliminated. Even worse, you could suffer a career-ending disability or pass away. By the time you reach your fifties, odds are you've experienced major life disruptions and seen this happen to people around you. Have a plan that considers this and includes emergency savings.

   • Robert and Linda had a timeframe for retirement in mind and expected it to work. Unlike Marie, they didn't think that much about the risk of what-if. Linda discussed it a little with her financial planner but didn't spend time dwelling on it.

5. **The most important questions about the future often can't be answered.** How much is "enough money" to retire comfortably? How much will I need if I have health problems? All financial planning, or any type of planning, includes assumptions because there are things we can't foresee. Like the butterfly effect—a minor change or one small assumption being incorrect can dramatically change the big-picture outcome.

   • How can you plan financially for an unknown future? In overly simple terms, here's the process: Start with what is known. Review your income, expenses, assets and liabilities. Then move to what you wish for or want to happen (travel, pay for grandchildren's college, etc.). Next, consider what you don't want to happen (run out of money, poor health, long-term care expenses, etc.).

6. **It's never just about you.** Life events have a ripple effect and impact people around you. The closer that person is to you, the stronger the effect.

   • When change happens, people instinctively think about how it impacts them. What does this mean to me? How will this affect my future? Then consider what this means to people close to you. Think about how those people would answer the previous questions. Then ask them how they're feeling and what they're thinking.

   • Consider Robert losing his job. Yes, everyone was concerned for Robert and how he felt. But they also had their own worries. Marie is closest to Robert, so the impact hit her the hardest. She was scared. Robert's job loss impacted her in many ways. Linda and Angie were worried for Robert and Marie but also thought about how it would impact them. A smaller ripple, but it still had an effect.

7. **Transitions often overlap and may create a domino effect.** Overlap can easily lead to being overwhelmed and confused. Transitions follow their own path, sometimes planned and anticipated, other times sudden and unwelcome. One transition may lead to a second one before the first transition is completed.

   • Consider the concept of multiple transitions from Marie's perspective. Robert loses his job, which shakes Marie's financial security. Then, Marie starts a new career. Angie announces she's no longer capable of living independently, while Linda retires early and travels the world. All of this happens within a few months, and Marie can't know how each transition might impact her life.

   • It's important to see each transition individually. Take time to identify the stage and needs at that time. Each transition may call for separate actions, and that's okay.

8. **Life will never be the same, and neither will you.** Major life events bring more significant changes. But even seemingly small events can have dramatic implications. Don't expect life to go backward and return to normal. Change eventually leads to a new normal. Your life may be similar in some ways but never exactly the same.

- Recognizing how much life has changed around you may be obvious (lost a job, moved to a new city, a family member passed away, etc.). But recognizing how you changed as a person is more important. Self-awareness is a lifelong challenge that requires time and energy. The payoff is more confidence in handling new challenges as they occur. Try keeping a journal to reflect on what just happened, what's happening now, and what you think about the future.

9. **There is no new beginning without an ending.** It's easy for people to look forward to the start of retirement after decades of working. Even people who are financially secure need to find ways to make life fulfilling. It doesn't just happen on its own. For many people, the end of job-related routines and relationships is traumatic. Recognizing that as "part of the process" will often yield a smoother transition.

10. **Transitions are like riding a roller coaster.** Even though transitions have defined stages, they include twists and turns people either didn't or couldn't anticipate. Be prepared to encounter surprise, doubt, and confusion that you have to work through. No matter what happens, you have more control than you think, and you can learn to exercise that control and shape the life that you want to live.

PART 2:

TRANSITION PROTOCOLS

The exercises outlined here are a repeatable protocol that can apply to all life transitions. Elements of these exercises have appeared in the story. As you work through the exercises, reflect back to incidents from the previous chapters.

THREE QUESTIONS TO ASK YOURSELF ABOUT TRANSITION

Life events involve uncertainty, and many aspects cannot be controlled. Yes, life changes, and it will never be the same. But you always have agency, or some level of control, regardless of the event. As you begin a transition, consider The Three Questions:

1. **What do I need to protect?** What do you hold so dear that maintaining it becomes a top priority? Examples include protecting family relationships, your current home, or a family vacation home where everyone gets together.

    a. Initially, Robert wanted to protect his time at home. He didn't want to travel five days each week. He valued his time with Marie. A little travel was fine, but not all week, every week.

    b. Marie wanted to protect their home. She loved her home and didn't want to move. She would figure out how to make the money work, as she always did. But she wasn't giving up the home she had raised her children in.

2. **What do I need to let go?** Letting go is never easy, but it is often required after a major life event. Some parts of your old life have ended, and you had no say in the matter. Other aspects remain but don't fit into your life.

    a. Robert and Marie planned on retiring in five years. Maintaining their lifestyle and staying in their current home depended heavily on Robert's current income. Without that income, which allowed maximum contributions to his 401(k) at work, retiring in five years was not reasonable. He and Marie needed to let go of that idea and come up with a new plan.

    b. Robert loved his previous job. It was prestigious, and he had become a respected manager after years and years of success. He'd start fresh at his next job and be the "new guy."

3. **What do I need to create?** Eventually, you'll explore your hopes and dreams and map out what you'd like your next stage of life to look like. It may take years before you can look toward a new future in the case of traumatic life events. Be patient and don't force this. Remember, transitions usually take longer than you want but not longer than you need.

    a. Now what? All of a sudden, Robert's routine and relationships changed dramatically. He needed to get out of the house and stay active until finding a new job. Isolation isn't healthy, but almost all of his friends were working during the day. What could he do? He needed to create new routines and relationships. Robert thought volunteering, even if it was temporary, seemed like the solution. He'd be around people, feel productive, and get back to ten thousand steps a day.

b. Marie also needed to create a new routine and modify her relationships. Now Robert was home all the time. Her world was radically disrupted, just like his. "Until death do us part" started to feel like "Until death, we're never apart." She needed a new schedule that included alone time and more time with her friends.

As transitions progress, The Three Questions should be revisited. Life changes in unexpected ways at unexpected times. People grow, and their answers may evolve over time. At first, Robert wanted a job with little or no travel. Then he changed his mind as his hopes of fully replacing his income vanished.

Robert and Marie had to let go of retiring in five years. The numbers just didn't work. That was reality, and they both accepted it. Then Marie got a job and things changed. Not only do the numbers work now, but she also has no interest in retiring. Robert can retire if he wants, but not Marie. Initially, she let go of Robert's target retirement date. Now, with her income, Robert may be able to retire when they initially thought. But that's his date, not hers. She's happy and sees herself working well into her seventies.

STAGES OF TRANSITION

In *Managing Transitions*, William Bridges wrote, "Because transition is a process by which people unplug from an old world and plug into a new world, we can say that transition starts with an ending and finishes with a beginning." In that book and in his seminal work, *Transitions: Making Sense of Life's Changes*, Bridges presents his three-phase structure for the transition process, noting that phases are not necessarily separate stages with clear boundaries between them.

Phase One: Ending, Losing, Letting Go

Phase Two: The Neutral Zone

Phase Three: The New Beginning

The Financial Transitionist Institute uses a similar structure with one significant difference: an additional beginning stage called *Anticipation*.

STAGE ONE: ANTICIPATION

In *Sudden Money®: Managing a Financial Windfall*, Susan Bradley presented a financial planning model for sudden money® recipients that introduced some of the elements the Sudden Money Institute and

Financial Transitionist Institute would develop over the subsequent fifteen-plus years. Part of that model addressed the *Anticipation* and the planning for a windfall from a life event, such as an inheritance, divorce, retirement, or any significant increase in your net worth.

Anticipation is when you prepare to make decisions that have lifelong consequences, such as where to live and whether to begin or end a career. The life event is expected soon, but some details are unclear. The exact date and dollar amounts may not be known. But the transition has begun. You start thinking about life after the event and what that means. It influences your decision-making process, and emotions are heightened.

During this initial phase, before life changes dramatically, emotional bookkeeping and financial planning are priorities. How do you feel right now? How do you feel about the upcoming life event? What do you think life will be like after the event? Do you feel invincible, like you can do anything? Or are you overwhelmed by the thought of being taken advantage of or making poor decisions? What will your family members expect now that your finances have improved (or deteriorated)? Then, dream a little and think about "what-if?" You'll soon have options that may have been unthinkable a short time ago.

STAGE TWO: ENDING

Considering that we have to deal with endings all
our lives, most of us handle them very badly.
—WILLIAM BRIDGES

Ending is what it sounds like: Some aspect of life has come to an end. It could be a marriage, the life of someone close to you, decades of working full-time, or living paycheck to paycheck. You may look forward and see the next stage as a positive change. Or you may be entering a period of unimaginable stress and hardship. Regardless of the Ending, there is always some kind of loss and some varying degree of grieving.

If Ending is your first stage—meaning an unanticipated event has occurred—Ending's initial work is absorbing the shock of the life event. Numbness often comes with the realization that there is no going back. Everything as you knew it seems to no longer be the case. For instance, women who are suddenly widowed say they "feel dead inside" and "like nothing matters." Sometimes they feel paralyzed by their inability to handle even the ordinary tasks of their daily life. And then there's the reality that critical items need immediate attention—paperwork, meetings, phone calls, and lots of life-altering decisions. It can be exhausting, both mentally and emotionally.

When someone experiences a sudden Ending, the first financial steps are assessing the immediate needs and resources. Start by reviewing income and accessible cash. Then estimate monthly bills and upcoming expenses. People need to know they're going to be financially okay, at least on a monthly basis, before they tackle important decisions.

STAGE THREE: PASSAGE

During *Passage*, you come to terms with knowing there is no going back to whatever you considered normal. Life has changed, and it will never be the same. It's time to adjust your routines and adapt to your new life. Rather than relying on old notions of what things should mean in your life, you create new ones. This can take years, especially for transitions from major life events such as retirement, divorce, or the death of a loved one.

Passage takes as long as you need to reach a point of clarity, along with a healthy amount of energy and enthusiasm for creating your new life. Feeling fatigued or like you're walking in a fog is normal. You may feel lost in time, as your identity has been compromised. The big questions for Passage are: Who am I? Who do I want to be? Self-awareness leads to self-exploration as you journey through Passage.

Passage requires patience. Be conscious of the desire to rush this stage. Both you and the people around you may think it's time to get on with your life. Passage can be messy and take much longer than you expect. This can be frustrating as you think, *Enough already; I need to move forward.*

Your journey through Passage may be your first. Your experience is unique, but the transition is not. Many people walked the same road you're on and have similar experiences. Peer support and resources are available, and accessing them is critical to your growth and well-being.

The midpoint of Passage is when you start thinking more about the future than the past. It's time to reimagine your future and reboot your life. The way it was is not the way it is, and the way it is is not the way it will be. Time to reinvent yourself and your life. You're ready to ask what-if questions and consider all manner of possibilities. Passage comes to an end as you embrace your journey and are moving forward.

STAGE FOUR: NEW NORMAL

The life event is in the past, and the life event and transition have been fully integrated into your new life. You own the event. It's now part of your story and identity. Through Passage, you have moved through the implications of the event and thoughtfully considered your options. New routines and relationships are established, and you're open to whatever the future holds. You've achieved the best possible outcome in your new life.

This is the time when you speak of the event and life before the event in the past tense. You can look back and see how things came together. Some aspects of your new life are more challenging, while others are better. You have an appreciation for what you've just gone through, how you've grown, and no longer feeling like a victim. Your increased resilience gives you confidence that you can handle whatever life brings you in the future.

THE DECISION-FREE ZONE (DFZ)

The Decision-Free Zone® (DFZ) is a proactive time-out from making any nonessential decisions. When you're in transition, especially in the swirl of emotions and physical responses, it often feels like a thousand things need to be done at once. This exercise aims to think about and prioritize what needs to be done by placing each action step into one of the following three categories. This decreases feelings of being overwhelmed and increases calm.

Now—action steps you feel are essential and need immediate attention (important and urgent)

Soon—action steps that are important but not as urgent as the Now items

Later—important decisions that need to be postponed until you have more information or more time to plan

During the Ending stage, you are still reeling from a life-changing event and are trying to make sense of what has just happened. Of this you are certain—your life has profoundly and permanently changed. In the middle of this, you will feel pressure to make one life-altering decision after another. The mental checklist keeps growing and evolving. What should you do first?

The DFZ creates a structure to identify what needs to be done, sorted, and prioritized. Some items are to-dos, while others are decisions. The first step is to list everything on your mind that feels important. Then, sort the list into now, soon, and later categories.

HOW DO YOU PRIORITIZE?

Once your list is complete, consider whether the task or decision is time-sensitive. Many financial and legal issues, such as paying bills, signing legal documents, or filing tax returns, have deadlines. After you create the list of what's on your mind, you can add any known or estimated dates. Do this after you create the list so you don't get bogged down with one decision. Once your list is complete, it's time to sort and prioritize.

Anything with an immediate deadline goes into the Now box. Include what needs to be done, by when, and, if applicable, who is involved. Example: Call your financial planner's office today to schedule a meeting for this week or next.

Creating the list can feel overwhelming, especially when the Ending wasn't preceded by Anticipation. But as you work through your list, you realize most items do not require immediate attention. Clarity and confidence grow as you work through the list.

* * *

Here is a sample DFZ for Robert. Marie needs her own DFZ. Robert starts by listing everything on his mind.

- How much are we spending? Where can we cut?

- Marie knows the budget. Need to ask her.

- Is my severance enough? What happens if my severance ends before I get a job?

- What happens if I can't replace my income? Is Marie worried about this?

- Do I qualify for unemployment benefits? How much and for how long? How do I apply?

- Did I lose my benefits, like medical insurance?

- Can my previous employer help me find a new job?

- How do I update my resume?

- What's the best way to look for a new job? I'll need a list of people to call and websites to visit. Does my previous employer offer help with this?

- Should I look for something temporary for now while I search for a higher-paying job?

- I don't want Angie to worry about us. Need to be sure she knows we'll be okay.

- Need to make sure Linda knows I trust and respect her opinion. She understands business and my situation.

- Should I cash in my insurance policy? Or do I need more insurance for Marie?

- Can I get to my 401(k) if I need it? If I take money out, how will that impact our retirement plans? Marie calls the 401(k) "untouchable." How will she feel about withdrawing money from it?

- Should we downsize our house? That would save lots of money.

- How would Marie feel about moving?

- Should we sell one of our cars or trade down both?

- How will this affect our plans to retire in five or so years? Will I be working until I'm seventy?

Many items involve what-ifs that can't be answered now. Some items appear on the list more than once, which is not uncommon during this exercise. Notice how financial questions can include a human component. Just like retirement, most financial decisions have two sides (human and financial).

NOW (IMPORTANT AND URGENT):

Who and what: Robert calls HR at his previous employer. Share all of the info with Marie.

When: Immediately.

Why: We need to know details about severance pay, benefits, and anything else the company offers.

SECOND NOW (IMPORTANT AND URGENT):

Who and what: Marie reviews the monthly budget once she has all of the information about severance and benefits. Determine what changed and what stayed the same. Then, separate fixed expenses from optional or variable. For example, Robert no longer has work-related expenses. The mortgage payment is fixed, but adding extra money to the principal (which Marie always does) is not.

When: This week.

Why: There is always room to cut in a pinch. Better to figure it out now since we don't know the future with Robert not working. We will feel better once we understand our income and expenses more clearly.

SOON (IMPORTANT, NOT URGENT):

Who and what: Robert begins the job-hunting process.[5] He updates his resume and learns which websites are popular for job hunting. Make a list of friends to reach out to see if they know of any open positions.

When: Over the next few weeks. Need to take care of the Now items first.

Why: Looking for a job isn't a twenty-four-hour project. Robert needs time to prepare, which includes updating his resume, networking, exploring job-hunting websites, and so on.

LATER:

Put off any major decisions that require more information. What if Robert has a good job four months from now? If so, he and Marie don't need to consider most financial items on the list. Were they planning to sell a car, cash in a life insurance policy, withdraw from a retirement account, or downsize their house before Robert lost his job? No, they weren't. Severance will last for almost one year, so there is no reason to rush and make drastic changes right now.

* * *

---

5   Why is job-hunting listed as "soon" and not "now"? Robert needs to be calm, not sound desperate or scared. Robert and Marie need to know their bills are paid, at least until severance runs out. They aren't going to be homeless next month if Robert can't find a job before then. In addition, Robert's resume needs to be current and thoughtful so it doesn't get passed over quickly.

Here is Linda's DFZ when the early retirement package is offered. Linda's list captures what's on her mind:

- The retirement package is offered. If I don't take it now, could my position be eliminated? What if they offer an even better package next year?

- Do I have enough in my 401(k)? Do the numbers still work?

- What if the market goes down like in 2009? What would that mean to me?

- What are the pros and cons of working versus retiring? Financial and lifestyle.

- How long can I stay away from Marie and Mom? How will they feel about it?

- How much money can I spend on travel each year?

- I don't want to make any big mistakes—been there, done that.

- What will my new routine look like? Will I be bored? What will I do when I'm not traveling?

- Whom will I spend time with? Will I enjoy traveling alone?

- What will I do first—how do I "start" retirement?

- I need to prepare to sell my house and buy a condo sooner than I expected. Where do I start?

NOW (IMPORTANT AND URGENT):

What: Evaluate the retirement package with her financial planner.

When: As soon as possible.

Why: Is the package good enough to retire now?

SOON (IMPORTANT, NOT URGENT):

What: Prepare to sell her house.

When: When she accepts the package and knows retirement is imminent.

Why: Moving and downsizing takes a lot of time and effort. Freedom to travel depends on selling the house.

LATER (NEED MORE INFORMATION BEFORE ADDRESSING):[6]

What: Working out a budget and calendar for traveling.

When: After decisions are made above.

Why: She is used to structure and planning things out. Having a schedule and a budget will make her more comfortable.

* * *

Here is Linda's second DFZ, triggered by her mother announcing that she's selling *her* house and moving in with Linda. Sometimes you can be in the middle of a DFZ and something happens. Then you need to start another DFZ and revisit the original DFZ. They will run concurrently. Linda's list captures what's on her mind:

- Oh no—what about me and my plans?

- When do I tell them about my news?

- I'll have to rethink the place I was going to buy.

- Do I need a larger place to make room for Mom?

---

6   Items listed as Later may or may not be addressed. These items entail acquiring more information before making decisions. Some of the info may present itself when "now" and "soon" items are completed. Or they require more time and thought.

- Will a larger place cost more? If so, can I afford it? If not, would Mom contribute to the cost of a larger, more expensive home?

- How does this impact my travel plans? When can I go? How often or how long can I be gone?

- Will I have less money available for travel? Can I cut somewhere else so I can travel how I planned?

- What is Mom expecting? Does she expect me to shorten my travel plans?

- What about Mom's needs? Is there something she's not telling us about her health? Will she need someone to look after her? Will Marie help?

- What else do I need to know? Should I talk with an attorney about my mother's affairs? I'm unaware of her details.

NOW (IMPORTANT AND URGENT):

What: Announce her retirement to the family.

When: Now.

Why: Linda's original plan to downsize probably won't work financially. Linda needs to understand what she can afford and what Angie needs.

SECOND NOW (IMPORTANT AND URGENT):

What: Hold a family meeting, with Marie included, and discuss Angie's expectations and time frame. Time to share details about health, finances, and legal matters.

When: In the next few days.

Why: Need to make sure Angie's affairs are in order. Angie is aging. Decisions should be made while she's able to be involved.

SOON (IMPORTANT, NOT URGENT):

What: Meet with her financial planner.

When: Within the next few weeks.

Why: Think through the house decision, and discuss the implications of Angie moving in with her.

LATER (NEED MORE INFORMATION BEFORE ADDRESSING):

The family meeting and home buying decision will impact the remainder of the list. Hold off on addressing the other items until more information is available.

REIMAGINING YOUR RETIREMENT

The future ain't what it used to be.
—YOGI BERRA

And neither is retirement. Walking away from work and earning a paycheck to live off of your financial resources is the old view of retirement. That may have sounded attractive when you were in the daily grind of work. Now people realize being retired opens a world of possibilities.

IT'S TIME TO RETHINK RETIREMENT.

Begin with rewording how you describe retirement, and let it shape your expectations and choices. What comes to mind when you consider a change in routines, relationships, and income? Is there a word that describes your mindset? Is it reinvent, recreate, or rewire? Retirement brings many changes and challenges. Learning to adapt builds confidence that you can and will reinvent yourself as life evolves.

What is your vision for retirement? It could include work, play, learning, or anything that is meaningful. Don't expect to have all of the answers the day you retire. Do expect to change your mind during

Passage, which can take years, as you grow into the New Normal. Ask yourself questions and spend time reflecting on what really matters.

Ask yourself: If I could do anything, what would I do? Don't worry about money or constraints. Just focus on what you think would be most fulfilling. This time of discovery, where you map various scenarios and possibilities, lays the foundation for prioritizing. Then, while considering your financial reality, determine how you can do what matters most.

Life is like a journey on a winding river. The water keeps flowing forward, but there are twists and turns along the way. Sometimes we're prepared for what's around the next bend. Other times, not so much. But we figure it out and keep moving forward. That's what people do when life happens.

Now think of retirement as a time when the river widens and branches off. Life now has more choices, destinations, and opportunities. Some are wonderful, while others need to be avoided. What will be fulfilling?

Start with the Three Cs.

COMMUNITY

The social element of retirement includes meeting new people. You can join a club, volunteer, or take a class, while connecting with people. If your job got you out of the house and around people, you may not have had to think much about community. Your routine and relationships were intertwined and driven by your job. Once you're retired, much of that may disappear and you may need to be more intentional about community.

CONTROL

As in being the boss of your income, health, and your schedule. Less constraints in life mean more control. When you're in a space of autonomy, you make decisions for the right reasons, and you're equally free to change your mind and make adjustments when necessary.

CONTRIBUTION

Having a purpose and being a part of something bigger than yourself are crucial to a fulfilling retirement. One study showed a link between purposeful living and well-being, including longer life, lower risk of disease, and better sleep. People with a purpose were more proactive in taking care of themselves, had better impulse control, and engaged in healthier activities.

DOES YOUR LIFE HAVE A RHYTHM?

Psychologists tell us routine activities with social contact that are challenging but doable and have measurable achievement are steps that can lead to satisfaction. Research by Mihaly Csikszentmihalyi indicates that these activities produce feelings of well-being and energy.

THE THREE Cs IN ACTION: SEEKING RHYTHM IN RETIREMENT

Rhythm can create a sustained feeling of connection and vitality. Is this what you desire for the next chapter of your life? If so, make it happen by intentionally adding activities and commitments with four components.

1. **Routine:** the pursuit is regularly scheduled but does not necessarily take place daily or weekly.

2. **Social:** the activity involves interaction with other people—some like you, some different.

3. **Challenging:** the endeavor helps you learn something new or meet a goal (personal or organizational).

4. **Measurable:** there is a way to measure progress, achievement, or success.

RETIREMENT CONVERSATION STARTERS

1. What does retirement mean to you?

2. If you had unlimited resources, what would you do?

3. If you found out you had to retire at the end of the week, how would you feel?

4. What about retirement excites you?

5. What would you miss from work?

6. What would worry you once you retire?

7. How would you define being "ready" to retire?

8. Are you looking forward to retirement?

9. Are you planning to work during retirement?

10. Is anyone financially dependent on you (parents, grandchildren, adult children)?

11. Have you explored how your retirement will affect your spouse/partner?

12. Do you have a clear understanding of your income sources and expenses?

13. Have you thought about housing needs in the future?

14. How would you describe your current level of activity and wellness?

15. Do you have a plan to live a healthy lifestyle?

16. Have you explored recreational activities or hobbies?

17. Have you explored meaningful activities like volunteering or taking care of grandchildren?

ABOUT THE AUTHORS

ROSS MARINO

Someone gave me a *Money* magazine for my fifteenth birthday. It was a gift that shaped my life. I read about companies' problem-solving strategies: here's what they're doing and why, solving a problem previously unmet. I was instantly fascinated with business and investments. The momentum continued in high school; I had a subscription to *Psychology Today*, and the science behind the human mind captivated me as well. I was perfectly aligned with becoming a financial planner someday, but of course in the 1980s we had no idea that field was the intersection of the financial and human sides. Before becoming a financial advisor right after college, I started my first business as a college freshman—being a DJ for fraternity and sorority parties. By the end of the first semester, I had hired other DJs and dived headlong into the business world.

The drive to understand people and money remains deeply embedded in me today. How can I help people make decisions? What's the best way to think things through clearly when there are multiple options? How do you figure things out when answers are subjective and what's right for one person isn't necessarily right for another? How do you plan for the future when the future is unknown?

In the late 1990s, I transitioned from offering general financial advice to comprehensive financial planning. To put it mildly, it was a rough start. An awkward bounce on a trampoline led to six years laid up with a severe back injury. I was forced to work from home in a small room above the garage; I couldn't sit down, and driving was a struggle. That prevented me from going to appointments or networking with people. The internet was barely a thing back then, so I had to figure out how to build a financial planning business over the phone in a rapidly evolving industry. I was also in the process of becoming a CERTIFIED FINANCIAL PLANNER™ (CFP®), but the injury derailed my plans. Everything I worked and planned for suddenly changed. One day I was anticipating the launch of a career, with a strategy in place to make it happen. Then the next life changed and I needed an entirely new plan.

Fast-forward ten years. Health had somewhat improved, my wife and I had adopted two amazing daughters, and my practice was flourishing. Then life happened, again. I found myself as a parent of a special-needs child and caregiver for my wife. Seemingly overnight there weren't enough hours in the day; I had less time in the office and more disruptions throughout the day. Eventually, I learned to work within my constraints, again. In the following years, I launched a company that educates and trains financial advisors and founded a nonprofit that creates jobs in Haiti.

The combination and timing of my challenges may be unique, but that doesn't make me special. Life happens to everyone, regardless of how much planning we do. I've lived it and seen it firsthand in the people around me. Yes, change is hard. You know what's even harder? Making life-altering financial decisions in the middle of those changes.

For years I read voraciously about behavioral finance, behavioral psychology, and change management, including William Bridges's book on transitions. It was a light bulb moment; I told my wife, "This is what matters in financial planning, and it's not being addressed enough. I have to help people understand how to manage changes in life and make decisions. That's the missing piece in our industry. I'm going to build my practice around helping people make financial decisions during transitions."

About six months into a path of educational learning, I stumbled across Susan Bradley's website. I had no idea she had founded an institute for financial planners, but I knew her name and had read some of her work. I rushed home from work and showed my wife the homepage on Susan's website, and we both lit up like little kids in a candy store. There it was: an institute that trains advisors how to help clients manage transitions. My wife said, "Isn't that what you want to create? Whose site is that?" I told her about Susan and the Financial Transitionist Institute (FTI). She said, "So you don't have to build it? It's already built? You've got to call her!" With a big grin, I replied, "I already did."

When I discovered Susan's website, I called her on the spot. I was familiar with her book, *Sudden Money*, but not with FTI. Through the inspiration of my own life challenges, followed by self-discovery and years of study, the FTI materials resonated with me. The missing piece in the financial planning industry apparently wasn't missing. We've been working together ever since.

SUSAN BRADLEY

As a young adult, I was offered a fantastic, and some would say golden, opportunity to enter the financial world by my uncle, a director at a major brokerage firm. It consisted of a surprising invitation to join him for lunch at the corporate headquarters in New York City. The setting was impressive on all counts, a large private dining room with commanding views in three directions and art on the wall that rivaled the contents of a museum. As he sat behind his beautiful antique desk, he described what life could be like if I became a stockbroker.

I asked why he thought I was cut out for his world. First, he appealed to my adventurous spirit, and he said, "Look around, you only see women as secretaries. You could be one of the first women brokers in the company." Next, he tried to build my confidence. He pointed to my natural communication and teaching skills, which he had observed throughout my childhood. As the second oldest of ten, I describe my birth order as a middle management position. Part of my job was to help keep order and teach my younger siblings how to say their prayers and swim. I assume these two survival skills still serve them well today. Somehow, my uncle thought this translated into being a top-producing stockbroker. I could not articulate why this was not a good fit. I just trusted my gut and said, "No thank you."

This meeting did spark an interest in learning how money works. I had a home-based business with hours of quiet time to do design work. I began listening to one of the early talk radio shows about money. The language of money became familiar; the difference between a stock and a bond, interest rates, which were double digits at the time, systematic saving, and financial planning. This is when I discovered the CERTIFIED FINANCIAL PLANNER™ designation. My gut said, "Yes, this is my new path to follow."

By 1982 I was a CFP® living in Florida in need of real-life training, not just textbook learning. Soon, I found an award-winning CFP, and I offered myself as an apprentice. It was a great deal for both of us. Rather than becoming one of the first women stockbrokers, I became one of the first women in financial planning.

After a few years, I began teaching a personal financial planning class at the local community college. Two of the local NBC newscasters were in one of my classes. The next thing I knew, I was a consumer advocate on TV. The station needed a segment on money and an additional woman in their weekly lineup. Then came my radio show on financial planning. Both lasted beyond ten years.

During the 1990s I taught the Kids Money Camp, a one-week summer camp at the Breakers Hotel. Next came retreats for women in Palm Beach, Florida, and around the country. Every curriculum I taught included a combination of financial literacy and traditional financial planning. That seemed to be the answer in every situation that came up until I had lunch with an attorney handling a class action lawsuit.

The attorney was representing three hundred women with medical complications due to breast implants. He told stories of the women making commitments and spending money in anticipation of the financial settlement. Red flags shot up in my brain. These women were future-spending money that may or may not come to them! I offered to help and wrote a quick white paper, hoping a quick dose of financial literacy would help. It didn't. The defendant filed for bankruptcy before the three hundred women had received a settlement check. As a result many of the women filed for bankruptcy.

While researching the white paper, I reached out for assistance, but no one in the industry—academic, corporate, CFP—had any information or a financial planning model for legal settlements.

I quickly realized it wasn't just these big, high-profile cases; my widowed clients, inheritor clients, and divorce clients experienced similar challenges. And it was astonishing to see similar challenges show up in my retiring clients.

Financial planning is logical. Stick to the process, make informed decisions, and things generally work out. That is until *life as you know it* gets turned upside down by a disruptive event. As professionals we witness clients going through life-altering events, but we had no process to address it.

In January 2000, *Sudden Money: Managing a Financial Windfall* was published. I had written the book I needed and wanted to read. It was a huge project for me, and I was ready to move on from being a writer to being an author. But as Max Planck, the founder of quantum physics, said, "When you change the way you see things, the things you see change."

My view of the financial planning profession was forever changed. I saw the human experience of these life events, not the financial details, as the starting place. Both sides, human and financial, were equally important and complex. The financial planning industry needed a new body of work for the human side. I quickly realized this wasn't a one-person job. Thus the Sudden Money Institute was born in June 2000. Fast-forward twenty years and our team built and continues to grow that body of work. The institute trains financial planners in five continents to be CeFTs (Certified Financial Transitionsists®). The curriculum is advanced, often described as a post-CFP® designation (there is no formal connection between the two designation programs). CeFTs like Ross commit to training themselves to be both their client's financial planner and their transition thinking partner. They help their clients manage life transition events, intending to shape change as life moves from one chapter to the next.

ADDITIONAL RESOURCES

Age-Proof: Living Longer without Running Out of Money or Breaking a Hip, by Jean Chatzky and Michael Roizen, MD.

Live Long, Die Short: A Guide to Authentic Health and Successful Aging, by Roger Landry, MD, MPH.

Retirement Reinvention: Make Your Next Act Your Best Act, by Robin Ryan.

Managing Transitions, 25th Anniversary Edition: Making the Most of Change, by William Bridges and Susan Bridges.

Purposeful Retirement: How to Bring Happiness and Meaning to Your Retirement, by Hyrum Smith and Ken Blanchard.

CPSIA information can be obtained
at www.ICGtesting.com
Printed in the USA
BVHW091557260421
605865BV00012B/2374